*All about Recruiting Salespeople*

# All about Recruiting Salespeople

## Alan Williams

## McGRAW-HILL BOOK COMPANY

**London** · New York · St Louis · San Francisco · Auckland
Bogotá · Caracas · Hamburg · Lisbon · Madrid · Mexico
Milan · Montreal · New Delhi · Panama · Paris · San Juan
São Paulo · Singapore · Sydney · Tokyo · Toronto

Published by
McGRAW-HILL Book Company (UK) Limited
Shoppenhangers Road, Maidenhead, Berkshire, SL6 2QL, England
Telephone 0628 23432
Fax 0628 35895

**British Library Cataloguing in Publication Data**
Williams, Alan
   All about recruiting salespeople.
   1. Salespeople. Recruitment & selection
   I. Title
   658.311

ISBN 0–07–707356–8


**Library of Congress Cataloging-in-Publication Data**
Williams, Alan.
   All about recruiting salespeople / by Alan Williams.
     p.     cm.
   ISBN 0–07–707356–8
   1. Sales personnel—Recruiting.   I. Title.

HF5439.65.W55   1990
658.3'11—dc20                    90–5706

12345 93210

Printed and bound in Great Britain by Page Bros (Norwich) Ltd

*For my Mother, Olga Walsh
to show I have used my 'O' level to good advantage*

# Contents

# Preface

'A wise man will make more opportunity than he finds.'

Francis Bacon 1561–1626

Having spent the last fourteen years of my life in sales recruitment and the past thirty-odd years in sales and management, it seemed a fairly obvious thing to write a book about the business of recruiting salespeople, especially as I spend a lot of my time writing, and McGraw-Hill was chasing me for a follow-up to 'All about Selling' which they published in 1983.

If you have bought this book because you have direct or indirect responsibility for sales recruitment, if you are in sales management, personnel or independent recruitment, you don't need me to tell you that there are never enough accomplished salespeople to satisfy the prevailing demand, irrespective of the product, industry or market-place.

That is the scenario in which most sales recruitment takes place; but as if that were not a big enough problem in itself, the difficulties in recruiting the right kind of salespeople are often exaggerated by insufficient knowledge of the skills and disciplines that sales recruitment demands, and by failure to continually give the process the priority it deserves.

The objective of this book is to provide sales managers, and personnel professionals who are involved in the process of sales recruitment, with a greater awareness of the skills, disciplines and market realities of recruiting salespeople. Above all it is intended to emphasize the real priority of recruitment within the total responsibilities of sales management. After all, few companies are prepared to reduce their revenue objectives simply because the sales manager hasn't managed to recruit enough salespeople, and sales management becomes rather pointless if there are no salespeople to manage.

There are many factors which affect the process of sales recruitment: the availability of candidates, methods of generating and processing applicants, company policy, training resources, remuneration schemes, and so on. Within the following pages you will find ideas and information that will help you in your endeavours to achieve the true potential of your sales team by sustaining a full complement of satisfied and successful salespeople. Getting the right person for the right job is an extremely difficult task in itself; but when this is compounded by the complex mix of characteristics, skills and experience that make up the successful salesperson, and by a shortage of supply, sales managers need all the help they can get. My intention is to contribute towards making the task a little easier and perhaps more successful.

Throughout this book I have referred to the sales manager as being the person vested with responsibility for recruiting sales personnel. While this is ultimately true, other people may well play a crucial role in satisfying the need to keep the sales team up to headcount. In most major companies this usually means the personnel department, which could involve a personnel officer who has been specifically designated for the job, or even the personnel manager. I would like to point out that in most cases where I have referred to the sales manager I could equally have used the title personnel manager.

Thank you very much for buying this book and, whatever your aspirations and endeavours, I wish you all the success you deserve.

Alan Williams

# Acknowledgements

Writing this book took a lot longer than I expected. Due to a variety of pressures, mostly business, its first draft was consigned to a drawer for a couple of years, by which time I decided to rewrite it. I hope you think it was worth the effort.

If it had not been for continuing but patient prodding from several editors at McGraw-Hill I guess this book would still be in the drawer waiting for all my good intentions eventually to have some kind of effect. So, thanks to them for their tolerance and understanding. Thanks also to my colleagues at Sales and Marketing Recruiters, The Sales Training Company and Psychometrics, and my associates in Europe and Scandinavia, for their support and encouragement. At least they now have some evidence of what I do when I sometimes stay at home on a Friday.

Many thanks also to Rosalind Jones for typing the first and final drafts of the book, and to my wife Margaret for her patience and support.

# 1.

# What are the options?

'Oh brave new world, that has such people in't.'

*William Shakespeare 1564–1616*

## Getting the priorities right

January can be a depressing month. The Christmas and new year festivities are over and with them much of the good will towards men. It's back to the survival game, with most of the winter yet to come. For salespeople and sales manager alike, the role is 'yesterday's hero', irrespective of how successful they may have been last year. 'That was good, now do it again; plus a little bit, or even a large bit more.' If you're lucky, you may work for a company whose fiscal year is not a calendar year and all the bad news doesn't come at once. Either way, there comes a time every year when all the counters return to zero and you have to prove all over again that you can really hack it. Of course, that's very much a part of what selling is about; the challenge of identifying a goal of achievement and going for it. If you cannot react positively to that situation, then you shouldn't be in the job.

However, sales managers very often have a particular problem on the advent of a new selling season. Is the sales team large enough to win the battles ahead? It is now that many sales managers begin to realize the importance of initiating the sales recruitment process at the right time. Perhaps they were so busy chasing their existing sales team and closing business in the hope of achieving targets last year that next year appeared not to exist; but now it's here. The seemingly impossible targets, inflicted irrespective of staff shortages or the fluctuation of international exchange rates, have been written on the wall: there's nothing in the bag, and to make matters worse there are too few salespeople to have any chance of making it. Maybe a few people had to be fired, perhaps some walked away, or possibly the size of the team is to be increased, or any permutation one cares to think of. Whatever the reason, the sales manager realizes that the sales recruitment process should have been initiated months ago!

It is also at this point in the proceedings that the learning curve between the arrival of the new recruit and the likely achievement of initial sales success is seen in its true light. After all, one cannot expect a new recruit to close anything other than 'bluebirds' in the interim period that consists of basic training plus the length

1

of the average 'selling-cycle'. At this time of year, more than any other, sales managers begin to appreciate that their newly acquired targets are only as achievable, and their own future as secure, as the number of salespeople they have on board to do the selling.

I recall an occasion one August, when my own company carried out a recruitment assignment for a major computer manufacturer. The advertising campaign was successful and after the preliminary interviews had been completed we had a good short-list of appropriate candidates. The company's senior management was satisfied with both the volume of applicants and the quality of a cross-section of candidates they met. Consequently, responsibility for processing the applicants was quickly passed to branch sales management. However, by this time it was September, and the pressure was beginning to build up for the sales team to close a number of significant deals before the end of the month, which also marked the conclusion of their company year. As a result, recruitment was given a relatively low priority. Time dragged on and the candidates became restless. Several of them changed their minds, some solicited the services of other recruitment organizations, as we could not ethically put them to other clients, and some began to pursue alternative offers of employment. Then, the company decided to re-organize for the new selling year, which created considerable uncertainty about the size and structure of teams.

More time passed and those candidates who remained concluded that the lack of progress was some measure of the management's decisiveness, and simply decided to stay put or accepted offers elsewhere. Suddenly, and not without some pressure from senior management, the branch sales managers began to rush around asking for interviews to be set up; but by then it was far too late. Every one of the worthwhile applicants was gone, we had invested a lot of time, money and effort for no return and our client's revenue expectations for the territories concerned had been set back by at least three months—revenue that would never be recovered. It probably cost them in the order of half a million pounds in lost income.

The total elapsed time from initiation to the end of the campaign was almost four months, whereas the whole process from short-list applicant to individual job offers should not have taken more than four weeks!

When we came to analyse the reason for the unusual occurrence of a completely failed recruitment campaign the reason was very simple. It was not the company, the products, the income package, the personalities or recruitment methods that were to blame: it was simply the failure of field sales management to give priority to interviewing and selection once the recruitment process had been instigated. There was always some other event that seemed to justify greater priority, until it was too late.

Effective sales recruitment is one of the most important elements of the sales manager's role. One only has to consider the profits that are lost because of unachieved revenues due to unmanned sales territories to realize how costly the failure to recruit can be.

## 'Ready-made' salespeople

Apart from the ethical considerations, it is to a great extent an illusion that 'ready-made' salespeople bring with them a significant amount of meaningful 'sales contacts'. Certainly one might expect an experienced newcomer from a competitor to get up to speed quicker than one who has never sold your type of equipment before. But equally, one with such limited loyalty to a previous employer is just as likely to leave his or her new one with the same lack of compunction, causing inconvenience to all concerned.

An important aspect of recruiting fully experienced salespeople is to understand their behavioural pattern within an operational environment. Those who are effective and successful (who are, after all, the type you hope to recruit) tend to impose upon themselves a type of self-conditioning whereby they truly believe their product and company to be the best within their chosen market sector. Consequently, they have equally imposed this belief on their existing and prospective customers alike and their business relationships are to a great extent built upon this very premise. That this conviction should at a single stroke be lost in one supplier and discovered in another holds little if any credibility. The trust between salespeople and their customers is not an overnight affair and is equally unavailable on a quick-transfer basis. An important question for the recruiting sales manager to consider is why a successful salesperson should want to leave a good job to work for another company in a similar role for a similar income package? After all, if you're a winner, your present employer will be very anxious to keep you.

From the salesperson's point of view, change demands careful consideration of the financial implications of the 'commission trough' and also the risk of not really knowing if the rosy picture the prospective employer has painted is really true. Then there's the people bit. Will you fit into the establishment of another company? Then there are 'futures' to be considered. Can you be assured that your new employer is still going to be in business this time next year?

There is so much insecurity in the process of changing jobs that a successful salesperson needs to have very positive reasons for change. Undoubtedly the most common reason why salespeople change their jobs is because their sales manager has suggested it might be a good idea! Of course, many seek a change of company for completely valid reasons. The most common justifications are ineffective sales and company management, inadequate product portfolio, impotent marketing strategy, lack of ongoing product development, unsatisfactory rewards, career limitations, and unfortunate personal relationships.

An essential skill for effective sales recruitment is the ability to qualify the credibility of the apparently justifiable reasons given by salespeople seeking to change their jobs, and to take the appropriate action. To do this efficiently, interviewers almost certainly need to have significant experience of sales management and selling rather than simply being professional interrogators. Otherwise, they will fail to identify the subtleties of candidate reactions to well-considered sales and marketing questions, and be deprived of the benefit of that 'gut feeling' of practised intuition which is always more reliable than face values. In other words the judgements of most personnel departments and recruitment agencies should be considered as no more than a reasonable guide.

Remember the golden rule, *when in doubt, don't.*

## Beware of 'guarantee-hoppers'

So you're under pressure from your boss and you're below sales complement; but don't let yourself or your company be forced into risk situations. Choosing the wrong salesperson (most sales managers do that at least once a year) costs a lost of money.

Beware of one particular type of candidate, the one who looks almost too good for the job: the mature experienced salesperson oozing charisma and articulation; someone who is well presented, with considerable presence and an impressive knowledge of the industry in terms of products and personalities. Such people are first-class communicators with an apparently good track-record. They appear to have a complete understanding of your market-place and products, and turn the interview into a sales call with a good opening and a positive 'close'. Yet in reality they have achieved little or nothing for past employers and will almost certainly do the same for you. Call them 'guarantee-hoppers', 'easy-riders' or what you will, they are in fact a considerable hazard for interviewers who have had insufficient exposure to this type of salesperson.

The reasons why they survive are twofold. Firstly, if your particular industry is expanding fast, it will be able to sustain both the inept and the inadequate. Secondly, there is no reliable interviewing technique for quantifying such old-fashioned qualities as industry, integrity, initiative and self-motivation. However, one positive clue to candidates' real capabilities is the nature of their chosen referees. If they are not direct superiors within their present or previous job, be on your guard. A surprising number of failed salespeople quote their local vicar, Member of Parliament, or a pearl-diver they once met in Hawaii!

When you have decided to offer a job to a candidate, be sure to agree pertinent referees and follow them up. If you can take up some independent references, so much the better. I am amazed that in practice very few companies actually go through the process of checking references. (This most important topic is discussed in greater detail in Chapter 5.)

If you have to recruit experienced salespeople rather than growing your own from the trainee level, then still look upon them as trainees, starting at a higher level. Do they look like a good ongoing investment? Do you have the resources to exploit their real potential and cover for their inadequacies? Will they fit into your existing team? If the answer to any of these questions is no, then you are exposing yourself, and the future of your sales operation, to considerable risk.

## Recruiting sales trainees

In my experience, the most effective method of producing new salespeople from inexperienced personnel is *vertical market training*. This is not a new or revolutionary approach: like most good ideas it is simply the application of common sense. However, it does bring a much quicker return for investment in new recruits than generalized sales training.

A vertical market, as far as I am concerned, is product specialization within a particular industry. For example, selling anti-theft systems to department stores, welding machines to motor car manufacturers, microcomputer-based accounting systems to estate agents; rather than security systems to all outlets in northern England, welding systems to the manufacturing industry at large and computers to potential users in the Home Counties.

Vertical market training is simply the process of channelling new salespeople into comprehensive tuition within a single product environment once basic sales training and the company induction process is completed, and then releasing them into a single industry as opposed to a geographic territory. In this way they quickly become fluent with the benefits of the product, the various applications and the needs and peculiarities of the industry in question, and gain a real understanding of how and from whom to get the required internal support for both their clients and themselves. As a result they avoid the confusion of the company's total product range and the unpredictable demands of a broad geographic territory, thus developing confidence within their confined area of activity, resulting in more positive and effective selling.

This approach also makes evaluation of performance much easier from the sales manager's point of view, as the issue is not clouded by the distraction of a diverse prospect portfolio, a multitude of applications within a host of different industries, a wide variety of clients, and the burden of the learning curve.

Using this method of training one should be able to produce a relatively fluent salesperson within a period of three to six months. If a new recruit has not made substantial progress by this stage, the sales manager should be making fundamental decisions about whether or not the person is in the right job. Within the following six months one should expect to see new business being captured and perhaps the sales trainee's product portfolio augmented and/or the range of market industries widened in step with sales achievement.

This means it is possible for the cost of sales trainees to be off-set by revenue within the first year of employment, assuming that the sales objectives are based on standard products which can be sold and installed on a fairly short 'selling-cycle'. That is most important!

In my experience, even fully-experienced salespeople, who join companies to sell their complete product range, can take as long as eighteen months really to 'get off the ground'. Contrary to common belief, one can often get a quicker return at less cost from a sales trainee by using the vertical market training approach than from a fully experienced salesperson handling the total product portfolio.

Vertical marketing is not a new idea. Some companies have been utilizing this controlled and positive approach for many years, though many have fallen foul of the realities of geography. However, applying this logical philosophy to training and the development of sales trainees does succeed. Nowadays, many companies totally dedicate their sales, marketing and support activities to the vertical marketing discipline.

# 2.

# The recruitment cycle

'The pleasantness of an employment does not always evince its propriety.'
*Jane Austen 1775–1817*

If the term 'management by disaster' applies to any aspect of sales management, it has to be the business of recruiting sales personnel. A recurrent phenomenon of the sales recruitment business is a demand for services from sales managers who give the impression that they have been struck by a sudden desperate need for salespeople that was utterly unpredictable. In many cases this is because they have started a new selling year on the assumption that all they have to do to obtain the salespeople they require is to place an advertisement in the local newspaper or telephone a recruitment agency. On the other hand, their problem may have been created by someone suddenly leaving the company's employment, with questions of 'did he jump, or was he pushed?' paling into insignificance against the cost of having a territory unmanned and the length of time required for a new recruit to become fully effective.

One of the essential skills and, indeed, responsibilities of sales management is the ability to anticipate recruitment needs in order to facilitate early action. While it is undeniable that salespeople do sometimes resign without warning, the greater proportion of departures can be foreseen well ahead of the event, if only for reasons of inadequate performance.

Recruitment needs related to business expansion are clearly more predictable, yet remarkably this appears to have little effect on the ability of many sales managers to take action before the 'eleventh hour'!

The cost of leaving a sales territory unmanned can be appallingly high, and while there are no truly effective means of assessing it accurately, one can gain an appreciation of the price involved by way of the anticipated profits that might be gained from the employment of a successful salesperson who achieves the intended sales target.

In the case of a supplier of mid-range computer systems for instance, a typical annual sales target for a territory would (at the time of writing!) be around £750,000. If we assume a typical industry gross profit of 50 per cent, then the cost in lost profit (if we ignore monthly fluctuations and the 'learning curve' of new recruits!) is around £30,000 for every month that a sales territory is unattended. That puts into better perspective the need for giving priority to recruitment, and goes some way towards justifying the high cost of advertising or using specialist recruitment organizations.

Surprisingly, few sales managers properly consider how long it actually takes to carry out a formal recruitment campaign and the time involved in getting a salesperson 'up to speed' once one joins the company. Having made the decision to recruit, many managers appear to expect people of the required calibre on board in a week or two and to be securing sales revenue soon after. This is an illusion: the reality is usually very different.

Let's ignore the approach of 'shopping around' recruitment agencies on the off-chance that they may have a few top-class salespeople scuffing around with nothing to do, because that is wholly unrealistic. Accomplished salespeople don't have to hang around on agency files waiting for a benefactor. They are the kind of folk who are prepared to find their own employment if the need arises. More to the point, the best salespeople (and those are obviously the kind you are looking for!) are most likely to be happy in their present job, or earning too much commission to afford to leave. These are the potential employees who need to be given some good reasons why they should go through the risk and pressure of moving to a new company. So, a more direct and active approach is necessary in order to stimulate their interest. The passive approach of an agency file is unlikely to access such people.

Whether you decide to use an external organization to carry out your recruitment or do it yourself, there are a number of fundamental steps that have to be undertaken in order to complete the recruitment process successfully, each of which is likely to take up a significant amount of time. Reality dictates that active salespeople are likely to be booked well ahead with business appointments, which means they will probably be out in the field somewhere getting on with the selling job. Consequently they are usually difficult to contact and seldom available at the required time and place. This has to be taken into account when attempting to gain an appreciation of how long it is likely to take to complete the process that will get new salespeople 'on board'.

To examine in greater detail the basic elements of the recruitment cycle and cover all the factors involved, I will assume that an external recruitment consultancy has been given the task of solving the problem, for their activity will include all the processes the sales manager needs to become acquainted with.

### Establishing the requirements

It would be rather pointless to go rushing out to find a new sales recruit as soon as the need arises without first considering the implications of the situation. Sadly, however, that's what many sales managers actually do.

Vital questions must be asked. What kind of person is needed, when, and from where? What training is likely to be required? How much will be the cost involved and how will the trainee be paid? What method of recruitment shall be used? And so on. Once these matters have been considered, that essential

document the *job specification* can be created. This demands careful discussion and consideration so that a clearly-defined profile of the required individual and the function to be performed are clearly established. Large companies have the benefit of being able to get an objective opinion from the personnel department, as well as a proper understanding of internal company requirements and external legislative obligations. Many a sales manager's recruitment ambitions have been shattered because he was not aware that they were contrary to company recruitment policy or in conflict with a transient 'headcount freeze'.
—*Approximate lead-time: 1 week.*

## Preparing the advertising

Advertising is not simply a matter of dashing off a few selected superlatives about the product, the company or the wonderful job opportunity you have to offer. Whether you or a selected consultancy have responsibility for creating it, careful consideration of its purpose and execution is absolutely necessary. (The creation of advertising copy is dealt with in greater detail in Chapter 3.)

If the advertisement is prepared by an external consultancy, it will need to be checked before publication to ensure that no mistakes have been made. No company can afford the risk of some faux pas, or even a glaring error, offending a client, upsetting existing employees, telling lies about the job, or otherwise breaching government legislation concerning racial or sexual discrimination and employment protection. Above all, the company needs to know and agree with what is being said on its behalf and with the way it is being put across to potential respondents. Writing effective and legal advertising copy is not easy!

Then, of course, the visual presentation of the advertisement, in the form of artwork, typesetting, etc, must be acceptable. Nevertheless, one shouldn't fall into the trap of hiring a dog and barking oneself. If an external advertising agency or recruitment consultancy is used, their creative scope should not be restricted by insistence on petty limitations.
—*Approximate lead-time: 1 week.*

## Response lead-time

It is easy to assume that once the advertisement is in the press, applicants will come pouring in within a couple of days or so. That is seldom the case.

The first consideration is how long it will take to appear. Perhaps a trade journal has been selected: many of these appear monthly, and bearing in mind that there will be a deadline for the receipt of advertising, it could take a month or even more before your advertisement 'hits the street'. Weekly or daily newspapers are obviously more able to give early exposure to your advertisement, provided of course they are not too heavily booked. There was a time when the *Daily Telegraph* was fully booked for many weeks ahead with sales and marketing job advertising on Thursdays, which is still their principal day for such advertising.

There are of course many national daily newspapers to choose from, but these tend not to have a significant readership of salespeople. Generally speaking, it is wise to expect a lead-time of between seven and fourteen days.

Second, there are the respondents. Will they all be poised there with bated breath, waiting for your advertisement to appear? No chance! The most likely people to read it first will be those people who are urgently seeking re-employment. They will be making it their business to be sure they catch every advertisement that appears. It is realistic, rather than cynical, to assume that a significant proportion of such salespeople will have failed in their last job. Then there will be those who just happen to see this particular advertisement when glancing through the newspaper and like the tone of it. As their requirement is not urgent, it may be days, even weeks, before they get around to writing or picking up the telephone.

Consider for a moment the real possibility of an advertisement in a monthly magazine where a potential candidate sees your particular advertisement in a copy he picks up from a client's reception area. It could have been hanging around for a month or more before he saw it and a further couple of weeks before he gets around to making contact. Maybe you had to wait for a month before the advertisement actually appeared. Ten weeks lead-time! An extreme example I know, but it does serve to illustrate the point that the period between having the advertisement ready for publication and making contact with every respondent is usually much longer than one might think.

—*Approximate lead-time: 2 weeks.*

## Setting up the interviews

In addition to the problem of how long it is likely to take all possible respondents both to see the advertisement and to respond, there is the question of availability.

Unlike most other types of employees, salespeople spend most of their time out in the field rather than sitting behind a desk. (At least, that's the way it ought to be!) Consequently, they are much more difficult to contact in order to fix a time and place for interview. In addition, they tend to be booked well ahead with appointments, particularly if they are involved in technical or capital goods selling where there is a greater degree of formality than in fast-moving consumer goods, for instance. So, immediate availability is unlikely with many sales applicants. On the other hand, they do have greater flexibility of movement than other types of employees, which can sometimes be a compensating factor.

—*Approximate lead-time: 2 weeks.*

## Initial interviews

If a recruitment consultancy is involved, they will have been subjected to all of the delays already mentioned, and will then have to proceed with the initial interviewing.

Clearly, there will be some overlap between the response of candidates, the setting up of appointments, and the interviews themselves. Nevertheless,

depending on the volume of applicants, a significant amount of time must be allowed for carrying out the first stage of the interviewing process.
—*Approximate lead-time: 1 week.*

## Short-list interviews

Most recruitment campaigns result in the creation of a 'short-list'. In some cases this will provide management with a second opportunity to evaluate the best of the applicants. If an external agency is involved, this is likely to be the first chance management has had to gain some measure of the quality of their potential recruits. Indeed, they may not regard candidates seen only by external consultants as truly short-listed material. (Though they should if their selected recruiters are doing the job properly!) This may lead to a wish for two interviews rather than one before getting to a 'formal offer' situation. Then, there is the question of their own availability. They are unlikely to have anticipated the need to set aside time for interviewing and find their existing commitments necessitate some delay before short-list candidates can be seen.
—*Approximate lead-time; 2 weeks.*

## Final interviews

Hopefully, the sales manager will get to the point where there are sufficient candidates of the required quality from which to select all the personnel needed, though in some industries this is highly unlikely. This inevitably necessitates a final meeting at which terms are discussed and agreed. Once again, the availability of the candidate is a key factor. Existing commitments may dictate that a week or more must elapse before the applicant can come back.
—*Approximate lead-time: 1 week.*

## Period of notice

The length of time involved depends very much on whether or not the new recruit is coming from a direct competitor. If this is the case, then the chances are that his or her existing employer will go through the process of persuading them that it would be in their best interests to stay, and if this should fail, ask them to leave immediately.

However, this is not a situation that your recruitment strategy can rely upon. The fact remains that you may have to wait at least a month, maybe three months, before the new recruit is released by his or her present employer.
—*Approximate lead-time: 4 weeks.*

## The length of the recruitment cycle

As I have already said, there is always some degree of overlap between the various stages of the recruitment cycle. Nevertheless, the timing and importance of recruitment is such, that the wise sales manager will always work on a 'worst case basis.

In those industries where there is a continual shortage of experienced salespeople, the cost of delaying recruitment can also be accompanied by the greater price of having nothing to show for one's efforts in terms of new recruits.

At best, when all the stages of the recruitment cycle are put together it will be seen that it could be some three months before the new salespeople, so urgently required, can actually join the operation. Unfortunately the implications of taking on new recruits does not end there.

## Sales revenue from new recruits

Having got the right salespeople on board, how long will it take before the company can expect to generate revenues from the efforts of the new recruits? A reasonable yardstick is to add together the introductory training period to the length of the 'selling-cycle'. (The typical period of time between first contact with the prospective buyer, and invoicing for the goods that have been sold.) As well as taking into account the time involved in such processes as getting to know the company, its products, its people and its politics.

The duration of induction, product and applications training can vary significantly from one company to another, but two to three months would not be an overstatement. The length of the 'selling-cycle' also varies according to the nature and cost of the product concerned, but a large proportion of products would fit comfortably in a time-scale of three to six months. That could mean having to endure a period of some nine months before new recruits could reasonably be expected to produce revenues that would, among other things, off-set the cost of their employment. It is at this point that the sales manager who has just decided to implement a recruitment exercise begins to realize that he should have started the process many months ago. Of course, there's a lot of slack that could be taken up within these notional figures by good organization and concentrated effort; but they are much nearer reality than many sales managers truly appreciate.

## The implications of economic recession

Economic recession obviously creates a lot of problems for the sales manager, but it can also provide some opportunities. It is at times like this that the power of positive thinking comes into its own. It's no good 'putting up the shutters' and hoping it will go away. That is both impractical and an invitation to stagnation and disaster.

Many companies are quickly reduced to a state of panic when economic recession begins to bite and revenues decline, or at least the rate of growth begins to fall. Desperate measures are taken in order to sustain profits. Research and development is curtailed, advertising is stopped and the number of employees, including salespeople, reduced, or at least recruitment is frozen. They seem to lose sight of the fact that the more the market reduces the more competition increases, and consequently the need for innovation, promotion and selling becomes greater.

From the sales manager's point of view, freezing recruitment is almost as bad as sacking the sales force; for as competition increases the need at least to sustain one's share of a reducing market is paramount. Therefore, the importance of having a full complement of effective salespeople increases. Similarly, the 'luxury' of tolerating poor individual sales performance is unacceptable. A fast-growing market and a shortage of top-flight salespeople is a comfortable environment for the inadequate salesperson. Conversely, there is nothing quite like a declining market for clearly identifying who the 'passengers' really are.

Even if the sales manager appreciates these realities, it doesn't necessarily imply that higher management will think the same way. It is therefore most important that one anticipates the kind of negative effect that economic recession might have upon one's peers, and give them an objective view of the recruitment situation before corporate edicts are announced and the process of reversing them becomes politically untenable.

No matter how tempting retreat might appear, the reflex action of 'battening down the hatches' needs to be resisted, for there is a positive opportunity to be grasped. A reduced and more competitive market-place demands the highest possible level of sales performance and thus the sales operation must be staffed with real contributors. This could possibly mean releasing some of the sales team and replacing them with the kind of salespeople who should have been employed in the first place, irrespective of the lead-time involved in getting new recruits up to speed. Who knows, such action might even achieve higher performance with fewer people. Now that would please the big boss!

## Looking for 'superstars'

Recruiting the wrong person is more apparent in selling than in any other job function because salespeople are continually measured by their results. One can hide an inadequate clerk or a lazy secretary indefinitely, but the failure of salespeople stands out in the sales analysis like punk rockers in a nunnery.

Sales managers are usually exposed to two significant constraints when it comes to recruitment. They have to bear the financial, political, and emotional ramifications of getting it wrong, yet they are seldom trained in the skills of how to select the right people. Evaluating prospective recruits is much more than an intuitive process. Even to be right most of the time is a creditable performance.

Yet these problems can be further compounded by unrealistic requirements and procrastination, which result in delay and all its ramifications. This is typified by what a client of mine used to call the 'John Barnes Syndrome'. This relates to the situation where a sales manager, rather than observing the realities of the candidates who are available, the price that can be afforded and the attractions of the company relative to those of other employers, looks for a 'star' who is prepared to transfer to this team for average rewards and limited prospects, thus solving all of its selling problems. When it is eventually seen how unrealistic this stance is, that such people are at a premium and typically cannot justify leaving their present source of high reward, and have better options if they did, the sales manager begins to modify his or her position. This can develop into a period of indecision about the kind of secondary alternative that is acceptable. Meanwhile, the candidates who were initially interested are no longer available and the sales territory concerned continues to be neglected, resulting in lost business that can never be recovered. The effect on total revenues is obvious to all, including the sales manager's peers who eventually begin to wonder if they could do a better recruitment job themselves, particularly in securing the services of a new sales manager.

The chances of ever recruiting a sales team consisting entirely of 'the right people' is virtually nil. There are always going to be salespeople with particular strengths and weaknesses that need to be constructively exploited and off-set. The very existence of sales management as a job function, must to a considerable degree be due to the unlikelihood of ever recruiting a team entirely composed of ideal salespeople. Surely, the main reason why a sales manager needs the ability to motivate and organize a team, is because its members have insufficient capability to totally motivate and organize themselves to the best effect. It therefore follows that the more difficult it becomes to recruit ideal salespeople, the more the manager's own position is justified.

Sales managers and salespeople alike often complain about the lack of effective sales training within their company as if to suggest that the absence of sales success is due to a relative shortage of such training. I know it sounds unkind, but as the old saying declares, 'you can't make a silk purse out of a sow's ear'. Selection of the wrong individuals cannot be cured by providing them with remedial sales training. The wrong salespeople will, in my opinion, always remain the wrong salespeople. In this respect recruitment is more important than sales training. One must get it right from the very beginning. The risk of simply getting the team up to full complement, yet failing to recruit the right salesperson for each job, must be avoided at all times.

Ideally, a new sales recruit will have a substantial record of sales success, as well as experience of your product in the chosen industries or applications areas. Having said that, shooting for perfection is a reasonable starting point, but a naive commitment. If you can get most of the skills, experience and human characteristics required, settle for that. Of course, this begs the question, 'What skills are most important—product, industry, applications or selling?' Well, there's no easy answer to that; it depends very much on the product. Some companies sell 'solutions to problems' as opposed to 'tools' with which the client can solve the problem for himself. The former undoubtedly demands the ability to speak buyers' language and understand their business if the problem is to be identified and the appropriate solution proposed. However, as a general rule, it is a much easier and shorter process to give people product knowledge than to teach them to sell properly.

In my opinion, the product has to be very technical and the market extremely specialized before such knowledge can be given greater than, or even equal importance to, established selling skills. The claim that good salespeople are made, rather than born, is a piece of overstated propaganda, which probably emanates from those organizations who have something to gain by providing the necessary training—and that includes my own! This does not mean that good salespeople can sell absolutely anything; there are definitely 'horses for courses'. Star performance in selling stationery does not guarantee similar success in high technology products. Many other factors such as the duration of selling-cycle, multiplicity and level of contact, educational background, intellectual capability, etc. have to be taken into account. That is why it is so important to initiate the recruitment process with a detailed job specification and a candidate profile, so that the sales manager knows exactly what to look for right from the very start, and how much flexibility can be afforded in terms of essential and non-essential skills, qualities and experience.

# 3.

# Methods of recruiting

'Character is destiny.'

*George Eliot 1819–80*

## Growing your own salespeople

The process of continual recruitment is a very important discipline for any sales manager; but the evaluation of prospective salespeople should not cease when a full complement has been achieved. When a complete team is running, that is the time to be selective and maintain a continuing search for outstanding salespeople. Let's face it, some members of the team probably won't make it this year, while others may decide to take their talents elsewhere. This kind of unavoidable attrition must always be taken into account. Having the names of a few good candidates 'waiting in the wings' who have already been evaluated as suitable material and can be called upon at short notice is a very valuable asset. In this way the sales manager can avoid the disruption and delay of having to carry out an unexpected recruitment campaign and the considerable cost of carrying an unmanned territory.

It is not very often that major companies like IBM come onto the market for salespeople. The reason is simple, they grow their own and appear to be surviving pretty well in the process. It is not coincidence that they have an excellent reputation for the quality of their sales training. Of course, sales training schemes cost a lot of money in the short term and it takes a long time to establish a continuing programme. However, it is possible for smaller companies to provide training for new salespeople by using external resources.

A few years ago I was involved in the creation of a recruitment/trainee scheme for a major computer manufacturer. The services side of the company, as was the case with many of their competitors, was experiencing considerable trouble in locating experienced sales personnel of acceptable calibre for both their technical and commercial services. We were asked to try and resolve the problem, and as a result of considerable interaction with the company's senior management, came up with a scheme for both locating and training new sales recruits. From the selection point of view we divided the range of desirable experience into three elements: Proven selling skills, applications and industry knowledge, and direct experience of using computers. The minimum qualification for selection was more

16

than three years proven experience in any two of the three areas. (While I now favour the use of psychometric assessment in a situation where human characteristics have a critical bearing on potential success, such evaluation was not used in this instance. See Chapter 7.)

The new recruits were deliberately chosen from applicants who were not currently employed by computer suppliers, which not only gave a very high response to press advertising but also generated many high calibre people who regarded the chance of getting into the computer industry as a major career opportunity. They approached the situation with an enthusiasm and open-mindedness that was most refreshing in comparison with the attitude of many salespeople within the industry who had become complacent in the relative security of one of the world's most successful industries. (Later on it was to be seen that such recruits have a much greater tendency to be loyal and enthusiastic company people with broader horizons than those who have 'been there, done that'.)

The basic training period was set at six months and was broken down as follows:

| | |
|---|---|
| Induction training | • The company. |
| *4 weeks* | • The full product range. |
| | • Computer appreciation. |
| | • Basic selling skills. |
| 'Bag carrying' | • Working on territory as assistants to established |
| *4 weeks* | senior salespeople. |
| Basic training | • The specific product area within which the recruit will |
| *4 weeks* | operate. |
| | • The specific applications area(s) within which the product will be sold. |
| | • Advanced selling skills. |
| Territory work | • Prospecting and new-account selling within the sales- |
| *12 weeks* | person's intended sales territory, but minus any existing accounts. |
| Assessment | • Counselling and appraisal with the appropriate sales manager, leading to a firm decision on whether or not the recruit is suitable material for sales success. |
| Sales school | • A single sales project from prospecting to final close, |
| *1 week* | lasting for five days and virtually twenty-four hours a day. |

This course needed a minimum of eight students to make it financially viable, so clearly it is not the kind of scheme a very small company could easily justify. However, it was most successful for the company concerned, and many of the people who joined the company via this project are still with them today.

Clearly, whatever the size of company operation, it is necessary to have the appropriate budget. It is sometimes difficult to persuade people at the top of the company that this kind of expenditure is justifiable. Accountants and share-holders are always suspicious of budgets which appear to provide no direct or immediate financial return. Well, accountants are not usually renowned for their vision and willingness to take risks; after all, their principal function is to analyse history. However, they usually appreciate a good investment when it is presented to them in the right way. That's what growing new salespeople really is. In times of recession and restriction, accountants are continually on the lookout for apparently unnecessary costs. Don't let them, or anyone else, be persuaded that investing in new salespeople is one of them; just talk about the cost of having an unmanned territory instead!

Even if your company feels it cannot justify the kind of training scheme I have described, that doesn't prevent you from pursuing a 'grow your own' strategy on a small scale, using a similar training structure. You may not even have to go outside your own organization for raw material as there are usually some selling aspirants around most companies; sales support people, engineers, customers and so on.

The capacity for product training is obviously available within your own organization, and selling training could be achieved by tuition from yourself, a period of 'bag carrying' with your senior salespeople and some well-considered and pertinent external courses. It's worth the effort; and just think how useful it would be to have someone 'on tap' when you suddenly have a sales vacancy. Apart from that, the money you save by not having to advertise or use recruitment agencies could more than off-set your training costs.

## What are the alternatives?

Even if you already appreciate that a vacant territory could be costing you thousands of pounds a month in lost revenues, the question is, how do you solve the problem of securing salespeople of the right calibre? You could be forgiven for thinking that many of the people who present themselves to you as potential recruits shouldn't even be in selling; for in almost every industry there are insufficient accomplished salespeople to go round. Recruiting effect sales-people is one of the biggest and most recurring problems of the sales manager.

So what is the answer? Unfortunately there isn't one; at least not in simple or absolute terms. However, here are some basic guidelines which should remove most of the uncertainties and hopefully solve many of the problems related to sales recruitment. Let's look at some of the recruitment methods that are available to the sales manager. There are five which just about cover the full range of practical and socially acceptable means. Of course, you can attempt to make direct personal contact with your competitor's best salesperson, you can 'shanghai' willing victims in their local pub straight after work, you can even molest stand-weary salesmen at the next industry exhibition; but these are not only self-demeaning but also rather crude and unreliable methods that do nothing to enhance the professional image of either the sales manager or the company.

The most common methods of recruiting salespeople are:

Word of mouth
Self-operated advertising campaigns
File search via external agencies
Recruitment campaigns via external consultants
Direct search via external consultants

## Word of mouth

Some companies occasionally put out a memorandum to the sales force offering a bonus to those who can introduce new recruits. More often than not such exercises result in failure because the idea is not promoted in a positive manner, with sufficient enthusiasm, or on a broad enough basis. Salespeople are not the only people who meet salespeople. It is just as likely that a secretary, an engineer, a manager or a clerk will have social or business contacts with people from the selling profession. So why should they be excluded from the search?

Of course, this is not the full scope of possible word of mouth recruitment in one's own company. What about the company notice board? This is a continual source of curiosity for even the most cynical employee. People are always interested to know who retired, got engaged, married or even sacked this week! They also like to hear about promotions, new product announcements, how the football team did last weekend, and the details of the knackered moped being sold (most reluctantly!) by the tea-lady's assistant. It is compulsive and necessary reading for everyone at some point in the week. So why not tell everyone they can earn money by helping someone with their career? Who knows, they could even buy a second-hand moped with the proceeds!

The same goes for the house magazine, assuming you have one. Maybe it goes out to the company's clients, who are possibly the best word of mouth contacts you have available. After all, they are likely to be seeing salespeople all the time, including those from direct competition. If they are happy with your company and its products, they will feel well disposed not only to recommending salespeople to your company, but also to providing them with reasons for joining it. However, such activity should not be limited to the columns of house magazines. It is far more effective to ask the entire sales force to make the situation known to every client within a given time-frame. You will be surprised how fast the word gets around. Your clients are likely to be more perceptive than you imagine when it comes to working out the good salespeople from the bad.

There is of course the possibility of giving the word to other salespeople during the course of the selling-round. Day-to-day selling activity usually brings the salesperson in contact with others in the same job, not just competitors, who could well have the kind of background and experience the company is seeking. There is no harm in finding out, whenever the opportunity for such conversation occurs.

This kind of imprecise recruitment will never satisfy a major manpower requirement, but it can be a very effective form of low-profile recruitment that can compensate for the continuing attrition that inevitably occurs within many sales organizations as the months go by. It also has some significant benefits. First and foremost, it is very cheap. A bonus of two or three hundred pounds is significantly less than one would expect to pay a recruitment agency, but would be most satisfactory to a sponsoring employee. Secondly, it can usually be taken for granted that such candidates will be of a reasonable calibre because the sponsor will be unlikely to tarnish his or her own reputation by introducing someone who is inadequate. Thirdly, such candidates are likely to have a good understanding of the job and the company as a result of prior conversation with the sponsor, and will come into the situation 'with their eyes open' which is likely to lead to a more positive interview situation. After all, a company can be given no better recommendation than the enthusiasm of one of its own employees or valued customers.

Of course, this approach can only be successful if your employees and customers are happy. No one wants to draw even an acquaintance into an unsatisfactory company or product situation. The sponsor is likely to feel much more responsible for considering the potential candidate's personal and domestic circumstances than a company ever could. Conversely, everyone wants to work for a happy and successful company, and if that is you, go out and tell the world. If it is not, maybe you should be reading someone else's notice-board, particularly if you need a moped!

## Self-operated advertising campaigns

Advertising is the most effective and widely used means of generating candidates. Yet many sales managers eventually abandon advertising in disgust, having spent many thousands of pounds without achieving any significant success.

Truly effective recruitment is not achieved by simply putting an advertisement in the press and awaiting a deluge of replies. Those companies whose own efforts fail, do so because they lack the flair and expertise for putting together the right copy and presentation, are unaware of the most appropriate media for their particular requirement, or fail to give the kind of response, priority and follow-up that is necessary to have any chance of success. Note that I say 'any chance'. No advertising, no matter how well conceived, can guarantee recruitment success.

It is no good simply advertising for salespeople in general in the same journal as everyone else and offering much the same compensation package as one's competitors. All you are likely to do is inherit failures from other companies. There are few justifiable reasons why an apparently successful salesperson should leave a good job, to go through the trauma of learning about new products and possibly new markets and applications, generating new prospects and getting them to the 'closing' stage, before finally getting back to the same kind of earnings he or she enjoyed with the previous employer.

### Guidelines for producing successful recruitment advertising

1. The presentation must be sufficiently eye-catching to offset the competition of adjacent advertisements. As a rule of thumb a browsing reader

(particularly the successful salesperson who isn't necessarily looking for a new job!) is unlikely to spend more than four seconds glancing across a page of advertisements, and that's how long you have to make visual contact.

2. The key points of the job must be emphasized; bearing in mind the aforementioned 'Four-Second Test'. Whether or not the reader is actively seeking a new job, the statements that will catch the eye are:

- Current job-title or the one to which the candidate aspires.
- Place or region in which the candidate lives, or would like to live.
- Remuneration equal to or greater than the candidate's needs.

Figure 3.1 demonstrates how these key factors can be featured within display advertisements. If these are not sufficiently bold to catch the eye of the potential candidate, your advertisement is likely to be disregarded by salespeople, other than those who are actively seeking alternative employment.

Most people who are considering a change of employer are usually less flexible about changing their domestic location than any other aspect of the job. The ramifications of changing the location of one's home, with all it entails in terms of removals, finding new schools, buying and selling a house, etc. are such that the job opportunity needs to be very special, or the individual's situation needs to be fairly desperate, before the horrors of relocation are seriously contemplated. While personal mobility is a fundamental part of being a professional salesperson, only fools and masochists will eagerly volunteer for the experience. Consequently, people who are seeking re-employment will be particularly attracted to advertisements that confirm the absence of any need to move house and home.

It may come as a surprise, but very few salespeople consider income to be the ultimate criterion for choosing a particular job. However it is an essential qualifier in terms of initial interest. Potential applicants need to know that the income package concerned will at least enable them to maintain their present standard of living.

It is most important that the statement of potential income is in no way ambiguous or optimistic. Overstatement can lead to both immediate and eventual problems; and there are no problems like personal income problems! Overstating potential earnings, by way of commission, bonuses, or whatever, has not only the obvious dangers of subsequent dispute, but also runs the risk of 'qualifying out' would-be applicants. They are likely to make the assumption that either the gap between their present earnings and those offered is too large, or that the company is attempting to mislead.

Basic salary should always be stated, as well as total earnings based on the achievement of sales quota. It can be a good idea to quote the typical earnings of the present sales force; it adds an element of reality and so increases the credibility of the advertisement. If the company is prepared to give a minimum income guarantee against initial commission earnings, that

## COMPUTER SALES PROFESSIONALS

***"A Man Is Judged By The Company He Keeps"***

***(17th century proverb)***

No employer could give greater personal kudos to the accomplished sales professional than this multinational computer manufacturer whose dramatic progress has been one of the biggest success stories in computing over the past two decades. To be part of this elite organisation is to be thoroughly trained, well rewarded, highly motivated and accustomed to selling the best products in the business.

Our client is the world's largest manufacturer of Single Architecture computers with a range from Desk-top to Data Centre. In the last year alone, corporate revenues increased by some $3 billion, with U.K. revenue in excess of £800 million and an average growth rate over the past five years of some 30%. That is success; success that demonstrates the superiority of the company's products, its research and development, its training, and above all, its people. Success that stems from a powerful sense of team spirit and an environment where consensus triumphs over autocracy.

We are looking for accomplished salespeople who possess the energy, confidence and enthusiasm to sell the company's full product range to both new and established customers throughout

**LONDON and HOME COUNTIES**
**NORTH WEST & NORTH EAST ENGLAND**

This calls for previous experience of selling computer based solutions for a Computer Manufacturer, Systems House or VAR within a Commercial environment. Opportunities exist within such markets as **Banking, Insurance, Building Societies, Retail, Travel, Transport, Distribution, Media, Government, Energy** and **Education.** Whilst direct experience of such applications arenas is desirable, it is not essential, as our client has all the training resources you (— or your customers!) will ever need. Relocation expenses will be paid where necessary.

Perhaps you have got to a point in your career where your present job has run out of challenges and few other companies can satisfy your personal aspirations. If so, this could be your opportunity to get back on the winning track, for all the ingredients for your future success reside here; limited only by the talent of the individual.

The rewards are many, including a company car of your own choice, stock purchase scheme, health insurance, etc., etc., plus a variety of other financial incentives that include a

**BASIC SALARY to £35,000**

For more information, please contact Alasdair Scott (London) 01-734 9776, Mike Suckling (Midlands) 0543-414040 or Alan Williams (North) 0925-445511. Ref: SSA/079.

**Sales & Marketing Recruiters**

Serving the Computer Industry from LONDON, LICHFIELD, WARRINGTON and throughout Europe

## AMBITIOUS SALES EXECUTIVES

***JOIN THE COMPUTER INDUSTRY!***

The computer industry is the most successful and fastest growing industry in the world. It's salespeople are the most highly rewarded of all and the opportunities for career advancement and personal challenge are enormous. Unfortunately, "Catch 22" normally prevents salespeople outside computing from enjoying these benefits.

This is a unique opportunity for talented young **Sales Executives,** with a record of outstanding sales success, to enter the computer industry. Superb sales and product training will be provided in the United States and the U.K.

Our client has been in computing for over twenty years and is a major supplier of computer peripherals, with a worldwide turnover of 500 million dollars. They are the undisputed number one in their marketplace. They now require accomplished people in

**LONDON & HOME COUNTIES,**
**NORTHERN ENGLAND, THE MIDLANDS**

Candidates must be bright, numerate, highly motivated and energetic, with lots of initiative and a burning desire to succeed in the highest echelons of selling. They will have at least two years successful sales experience, in such markets as Business Equipment, Engineering or Scientific Products, Insurance, Technical Services, Automotive or FMCG. Successful applicants are unlikely to be older than 30.

An attractive remuneration package will provide first year on-target earnings of up to

**£20,000 + COMPANY CAR**

plus many fringe benefits, including Health Assurance, Pension and Life Assurance.

Please contact Alasdair Scott or Mike Harris (London) 01-734 9776, Mike Suckling (Midlands) 0543-414040, Alan Williams (North) 0925-445511. Ref: SSP 079.

**Sales & Marketing Recruiters**

Serving the Computer Industry from LONDON, LICHFIELD, WARRINGTON and throughout Europe

**Figure 3.1** Recruitment consultancy advertisements

should also be included; as should a company car if that is part of the deal. Special rewards like profit-sharing, share-options, health insurance and such, should not be overlooked.

One final point to remember, be sure that the kind of money you are offering in the advertisement will not create any problems with your existing sales team, or indeed throughout the company in general.

3.  The principal benefits of the job should be highlighted. Every worthwhile job has features that make it desirable, and more often than not, special elements can be identified which make the job more attractive than competitive opportunities. Overseas travel, early promotion, unusually high earnings, and so on. These must be made apparent in your advertising copy. If one outstanding benefit can be identified that emphasizes the pertinence of the job to the targeted recruit, then this should be particularly emphasized.

    The announcement of a company's achievements, market stature, attitudes, etc. can often stimulate people who are not actually active in the job-hunting scene to respond to advertising. It may be that working for the market leader sounds appealing; perhaps they are not too happy about their company's attitude towards research and development, or whatever. The important thing is, if you have something really special to say about your company or your product, then tell the world. After all, your competitors won't say it for you!

4.  The advertising copy should be the truth, the whole truth, and nothing but the truth. Over-ambitious claims, descriptions and promises can soon become a millstone around the sales manager's neck, leading to discontent and demotivation.

    Such bold and emotive statements as 'Excellent Career Prospects' or 'Double Your Present Earnings', must be avoided at all costs if they really mean 'You will have as much chance of being promoted as the other 50 salesmen hoping for the same thing' or 'Our targets are twice as high as those of our competitors'. Make no mistake, if the candidate doesn't realize the truth at the interview stage, he certainly will when he gets on board.

5.  Be precise about the kind of applicants you require, but avoid the trap of focusing exclusively upon the ideal candidate. Such people seldom exist; and would such perfect beings come and work for you anyway? In other words, don't allow your advertisement to disqualify those people who are not precisely what you are looking for but worth considering. For example, only specify age limitations if they are absolutely essential. On the other hand, do state any qualifications that may be absolutely essential in terms of product knowledge, extent of selling experience, etc.

    While there is no point in processing completely unsuitable applicants, it is far better to delay disqualifying applicants until you have had the chance to speak to them over the telephone or read their curriculum vitae. There is always a danger that candidates who believe their qualifications to be marginal, or who don't realize they have extra strengths to compensate for apparent weaknesses, will not bother to respond. It is far better to leave the basic selection process until the nature of the response is known. It could be that the quality and quantity of response will make it necessary to modify one's demands. Having said that, one must always be conscious of choosing the right person for the job, rather than merely selecting the best of the applicants.

6. Consider the use of both trade and national press. If specific skills or industry experience is required, then there could well be a trade journal that directly addresses it. Of the national newspapers, the *Daily Telegraph* has a well-established reputation for generating a good response from salespeople. Regional newspapers should be borne in mind in terms of their typical readership. *The Sunday Times* appears to be the most effective of the weekly newspapers for sales and management jobs.

   It is also worth considering the use of local radio or off-peak television. The costs vary considerably; but, depending on the number of recruits needed and the type of candidate being sought, both have something to offer. Local radio has the potential for being very effective, particularly in an age where very few salespeople are without a car radio.

7. The cost of press advertising is extremely high, so it needs to be considered carefully. The trick is to choose the smallest size that is strong enough and big enough to catch the eye when surrounded by competitive advertisements. Press research has indicated that the minimum area likely to survive the impact of surrounding advertisements is 48 column centimetres. (E.g. 16 centimetres by 3 columns, 12 centimetres by 4 columns.)

8. Every applicant would like to think that the job he or she is considering will increase their skills and personal value in the marketplace. To a great extent, this depends on the existence of sales, product and applications training as well as identifiable opportunities for career advancement. If such possibilities exist, be sure to state them very clearly.

Job advertising should, wherever possible, utilize the services of a professional artwork studio so that the presentation establishes a good image and has the best possible chance of catching the eye of potential recruits.

One simple but effective device is 'reversing-out' the advertisement so that it appears white-on-black. The mass of black will tend to dominate adjoining displays. The use of powerful and relevant illustrations can also enhance the power of an advertisement.

The advertising copy must not contravene the Sex Discrimination Act. Many newspapers and journals insist that, irrespective of the wording of any advertisement, the term 'These jobs are available to both men and women', or a statement to the same effect, should appear. This ensures that there is no misunderstanding in terms of equal opportunities for potential employees.

## File search via external agencies

While the terms 'recruitment agency' and 'recruitment consultancy' tend to be used as if they mean the same thing, there is a significant difference between the functions they normally perform; though some organizations are able to provide both services.

The basic function of a recruitment agency is basically to match files of jobs with files of people, and vice versa. Employers supply them with details of their current vacancies and the kinds of people they wish to interview. Similarly, those who are seeking employment provide details of their qualifications and experience, together with a description of the kind of employment they would prefer. Usually, this information is gathered from face-to-face interviews. On other occasions it may be extracted from application forms, the applicant's own curriculum vitae, or even gathered over the telephone. Standards can vary considerably. The agency is basically a 'matching' service operating on the same basis as a dating bureau.

In contrast, the role of a recruitment consultancy is to work with the employer to provide comprehensive advice and assistance on every aspect of the recruitment process. This includes the specification of the job, advising on suitable remuneration, identification of suitable candidates, the creation of a practical and continuing recruitment strategy, and so on. This could result in a recruitment campaign being carried out by the consultancy on the employer's behalf, possibly in the form of advertising or direct-search methods.

At first sight the recruitment agency may appear to be the most convenient alternative to the sales manager who has an urgent need to recruit a salesperson or two. After all, the manager has the vacancies, they've got the people. What could be simpler? Well, unfortunately, the best salespeople (and presumably those are the candidates you prefer!) don't sit around waiting, like Micawber, for something to turn up. Salespeople with good track-records have too many other options, such as press advertisements, direct approaches from 'headhunters' and the initiative to approach directly the companies that appeal to them as potential employers.

In the course of my own recruitment activities, I constantly come across sales managers who have devoted their recruitment activity to 'shopping around the agencies', living in constant hope that the right candidate is bound to show up eventually. Unfortunately, 'eventually' can mean many months of lost revenue that will never be regained.

As I have already emphasized, the cost of an unmanned sales territory is, to all intents and purposes, equal to the value of the profit that should be made from the targeted revenue. This should be borne in mind when giving low priority to recruitment, or attempting to 'do it on the cheap'.

Nevertheless it is always worth contacting a few reputable agencies just in case they have any suitable candidates. Perhaps a 'drop-out' from some other company's recruitment campaign. If they have, this could be the means of a quick solution and minimizing lost revenues. The important thing is to move quickly into alternative means of recruitment once it is established that candidates of the right calibre are not immediately available.

One of the big problems that can come about from using any other than the best and most experienced agencies, is the time that can be wasted on interviewing inappropriate or inadequate candidates. This usually happens either because the sales manager is not absolutely clear about the job specification and the profile of the kind of applicant required, or because the agency simply does not have the skills and experience to completely understand the requirement. The sales manager must be very precise about his or her needs if endeavours to recruit effective sales personnel are to be successful.

## Recruitment campaigns via external consultants

By and large a recruitment consultancy carries out much the same process as one might perform for oneself. Their business is personnel selection. The main differences should be the availability of superior copy-writing skills, possible access to discounted advertising, the provision of client anonymity, and above all, the ability to handle response with the kind of urgency, commitment and understanding that one would wish for oneself. Recruitment companies are not typically more discerning or perceptive than the average sales or personnel manager. Their interviewing technique ought to be more polished, but they are no more likely to identify inadequacies such as dishonesty and laziness than oneself; no less susceptible to being seduced by smooth talking 'guarantee-hoppers'! The real strength of external consultants is their devotion to the recruitment process, in contrast to the sales manager who has too many demands from the sales team, clients and other business situations to give full attention to recruitment for prolonged periods of time. (This is similarly true of most personnel managers who also have many disparate demands upon their time.)

In most expanding industries, accomplished salespeople are extremely difficult to recruit, and those who decide to change employer are usually very fickle about whom they will speak to and the effort they are prepared to make in pursuit of an advertised job opportunity. A large proportion of potential candidates make only one attempt to make contact with an advertiser, perhaps on impulse. If there isn't a prompt response to their telephone call, the chances are that they will not get around to trying again. The high cost of advertising and the even greater cost of unmanned sales territories makes it essential that no potential candidate is lost through lack of ability to respond positively whenever such unpredictable calls occur.

One of the biggest mistakes made by sales managers, and for that matter personnel managers, is to consider the use of an external recruitment organization as a 'one-way' process.

'I have subcontracted the task of recruiting new salespeople to a recruitment consultancy. So I can forget about it until such time as they send me a short-list of candidates for interviewing.'

That is an extremely unrealistic stance. Total involvement is essential throughout the recruitment cycle if the exercise is to have any chance of succeeding. You must be constantly in touch with events in order to ensure that your needs are being given the priority they deserve and that you are available to provide the level of support and prompt reaction that the transient availability of accomplished salespeople demands.

## Essential disciplines for successful recruitment

There are a number of important factors on which the success of any sales recruitment campaign is entirely dependent, whether it is self-operated or in partnership with an external recruitment company.

- Candidates short-listed by the consultancy must by seen immediately. Delay increases the risk of competition from other companies and similarly interested parties.
- Try to speed up assessment and selection by limiting the process to a maximum of two interviews. Two interviewers at once can be a very effective means of increased perception and reduced investment in time.
- Remember the interview must be a two-way sell. If you don't highlight the features and benefits of working for your company, who will? Your competitors will certainly be extolling the benefits of working for them!
- The interviewer must totally understand the job specification. It's no good sub-contracting the task of interviewing to subordinates if they are not completely fluent with every aspect of the job opportunity. That's what the candidate has come to find out. Anything less can only lead to a loss of credibility for the sales manager and the company.
- Do not limit the search to the ideal candidate. Such people are seldom available when you need them; and could you really attract them if they were? A lot of time and revenue can be lost in finding out that many of the skills and much of the knowledge required can soon be learned and that the most enthusiastic candidates are those who see your job as a step up, rather than a step sideways.
- There must be continuity of action throughout the selection process. The candidate is more likely to assume the lack of progress to be disinterest rather than pressure of business.
- Remember that candidates' primary concerns are for their family and themselves rather than the best interests of potential employers. So, don't expect them to hang around and ignore other opportunities until you find time to make up your mind.
- If the company's administrative mechanism isn't sufficiently flexible to issue a formal offer of employment right away, then send a 'letter of intent' to put the candidate at ease until it can. That will show you really do intend to make a job offer, and it will not be assumed that no news is bad news.

27

- Remember that as the period of assessment and selection increases in duration the chance of successful recruitment declines.
- Bear in mind that a recruitment campaign from initiation to getting the required people on board could take well over ten weeks. (Which usually means you should have started at least a couple of months ago!)

Some recruitment consultancies have more to offer than others. Price is certainly not a basis on which to make a judgement, for most operate within a close range of fees. The major differences are that some really understand your problem because they have direct experience of selling, perhaps even in your industry. Consequently, they have professional credibility with your candidates and really know about generating and assessing them.

It is most important to select the right consultancy where you can establish a positive understanding of your present requirements as well as creating a continuing relationship in the context of your future needs. The chances are that your requirements won't be completely satisfied with the initial campaign. So, having someone who knows what you are looking for and is constantly searching on your behalf is worth a lot. This kind of relationship can often bear more fruit than the original advertising.

Perhaps the biggest benefit from using a recruitment consultancy is the opportunity of using time to greater effect. By that, I don't mean just the time that can be saved on the initial interviewing: that is relatively easy to quantify. The most unsatisfactory utilization of time when running your own recruitment campaign for salespeople is the necessity of being around just in case someone worthwhile should telephone. Secretaries, or whoever happens to be in the office at the time will not do. Good salespeople are in many ways prima donnas, and when they call it is as if they are calling a prospective customer, and naturally they want to speak to the boss. If the manager isn't there the chances are they won't get around to calling again. Prima donnas don't write letters either!

On the other hand, irrespective of whether or not you are running your own recruitment campaign, you can't afford to hang around just in case a good candidate might call; there are too many other important things to do. Sales managers' other responsibilities simply do not allow sufficient time for carrying out recruitment campaigns effectively, even if they have all the necessary expertise to do so.

Some sales managers may have access to a personnel department with the means to carry out interviews on their behalf. The problem is that the best candidates are not particularly keen to spend their time dealing with anyone other than the person they could be working for. After all, if the applicant and the manager don't 'hit it off', interviews with anyone else are pointless. Subsequent interviews with whoever is deemed to be appropriate are tolerable, but the initial contact needs to be with the line-manager concerned.

Another benefit to be gained from using a specialist sales recruitment consultancy is the availability of expertise that may not be available within your own organization. If press advertising is to be utilized, then a high level of copy-writing skill is essential. This medium is too expensive to afford getting it wrong. A knowledge of the specialized trade press is also important when you require a particular application industry or market skill. The ability to consider a wide range of possible venues is an essential ingredient of successful recruitment advertising. The acid test is in the advertising copy the agency presents for your approval. Whatever you do, don't let them go to press without seeing it yourself, and also consider whether you could do better yourself. If so, ask the agency to do it again. If you're still not satisfied after the second shot; try someone else.

The degree of personnel assessment skills within a particular consultancy is rather more difficult to quantify. Incompetence in this area is usually discovered after the event. However, a reasonable guide is the kind of information that is supplied as a result of candidate interviews. That will provide some measure of how much trouble is taken in assessing prospective employees. If the document does not give you a clear picture of the person's experience and achievements in direct context with the job requirement, highlight the candidate's career development to date, suggest the most appropriate courses for future develop-ment and give you a real insight into the person concerned, then the chances are they have not truly evaluated the candidate. Bearing in mind how difficult it is to select the right people and the cost of getting it wrong, you need all the help you can get. That's the kind of skill you should be getting for your money from any professional recruitment consultancy.

Another hidden benefit from using a recruitment consultancy is establishing a contact with the market of currently available candidates. Once a consultancy regards you as an established client and develops a real awareness of your needs, they will begin to identify candidates new to their organization who are in your particular mould.

Anonymity is another significant benefit for many companies. It is amazing how many salespeople have irrational preconceived ideas about other companies, particularly competitors. This is typically a problem for the larger companies. The smaller ones often have the problem of no real identity at all and therefore have little appeal to many would-be applicants. In both cases the problem is getting the right message to the potential recruit, rather than being unjustifiably qualified out at the advertisement level.

## Direct search via external consultants

One of the most significant differences between advertising-based recruitment and direct search is the calibre of the typical candidate. In effect, people who respond to advertising 'select' themselves, and many are likely to be motivated more by wishful thinking than by having relevant qualifications. On the other hand, those people who are found by direct approach are usually pre-qualified in accordance with a definitive job specification before the search consultant even makes contact with potential candidates. More often than not, the consultant is only dealing with people who are not actively engaged in seeking re-employment, because they are currently successful in their job. Consequently, the calibre of candidates is usually higher than achieved from advertising, which inevitably includes people who are on the job market because they have failed in their most recent employment.

Direct search is not the kind of recruitment a company will normally wish to carry out itself. It is a very time-consuming process, which requires painstaking and well-informed research, and is not without its political problems. However, it can be said, from the employer's point of view, that the actual process used by external recruiters is irrelevant, providing it generates short-listed candidates of the required calibre. This may be so, but failure to find the right person for the job (not just the best of the applicants, as I have stated elsewhere in this book) can leave the employer with a significant advertising bill. This is likely to be considerably more expensive than a retainer fee, or even no cost at all if a 'no cure, no pay' 'contingency' search company is involved. Nonetheless, it is the probability of higher quality and more relevant candidates that attracts many companies to the 'headhunter'.

'Headhunting' has become a popular generic term related to the business of recruitment. In reality, it is not a suitable or even accurate description of the various types of activities involved in recruiting. It is rather an expression that exclusively applies to direct search; the process of initiating candidates by making direct personal contact. 'Headhunting' is something quite apart from agency and advertising-based recruitment, where the process of candidate generation is to some degree passive, being dependent on the credibility and professional reputation of the advertiser and the persuasive power of its message. It is as far from agency- and advertising-based recruitment, as the hunter is from the skinner; one acts, the other reacts. Whether carried out by a large-scale professional organization or by a solo recruiter, the basic methodology of locating candidates by direct search is radically different from the means used by recruitment agencies or advertising-based consultancies.

Direct search is a topic that can provoke extreme emotions among employers and employees alike. While some praise the effectiveness and apparent simplicity of the process, others regard it to be unethical and damaging to company interests. I have to say that I do not regard it as a method of recruitment wholly beyond reproach. Direct search for me runs a very narrow professional course that can easily be compromised by the slightest deviation in ethics of the individual search consultant or recruitment organization. Therefore, stringent operational procedures and working guarantees are essential if a company's reputation is to be sustained and its services relied upon.

I had a very interesting conversation with a direct-search consultant in the United States who made the point that by and large the attitude of senior management towards 'headhunting' is hypocritical. While they value direct search as a convenient process for developing their own careers, they consider it unreasonable for their subordinates to enjoy the same benefit. My experience is that they don't really believe it to be any less fair for their people to be subject to direct approach than for themselves. What they do know, is that it is nice and often rewarding to be approached, but often inconvenient and expensive when it results in the departure of their own people.

In order to see both sides of the arguments for and against direct search, let's view the process through the eyes of someone who is basically against it.

Many companies are from time to time attracted by the apparent simplicity of direct search. (That's what they call it when you take an employee from some other company.) You simply state the kind of person you want, they find out where he is (probably working for one of your competitors!) and persuade him to come and talk to you about your particular job vacancy. What could be more effective? What could be easier? Unfortunately, you are not the only company with such a need, or considering direct search. Your competitors are possibly in the market too. So, what do they do? They also go to a recruitment company specializing in headhunting (that's what it's called when someone takes one of your employees!), and guess whose company will be on their shopping list? It's like taking out a contract with a hired assassin. 'Remove that person. Here's your front-money; you get the rest when the job is completed!' The vacuum it creates and the inconvenience it causes is someone else's problem. Simply provide your chosen 'hit-man' with a description of the target candidate, and off he goes in search of unsuspecting but seldom unwilling victims. The problem is, today's client has a habit of becoming tomorrow's victim.

After all, headhunting salespeople is easy, isn't it. You just contact the telephone operator of the appropriate branch of a relevant company in the right market sector and ask for some names. Being accustomed to people phoning with vague requests for product information and names of salespeople, and knowing how important it is to be helpful to people who make enquiries, when asked 'Who's your salesperson for Birmingham?', the operator is usually keen to help.

Who can resist the ego boost of a letter or telephone call which suggests that you have been 'identified' as the right person for an important, challenging and highly rewarded job? It confirms the under-utilized talent and potential you had suspected all along. It is a glimpse of greener fields and jam today rather than tomorrow. Only a fool, it seems, would say 'No thank you, I'm not interested'. After all, the chance may never come again! It costs nothing to talk. Flattery is a very potent weapon. More often than not the target candidate is hooked without even a glance at the bait. It's 'game, set and match' before you can say 'guarantee-hopper'.

So much for the cynic, but I have to say that there is a type of headhunter I find particularly untenable; and that is the 'roll over' recruiter. This is the direct searcher, usually operating single-handed, who has an established file of candidates from a variety of sources. Some may have been taken from agencies with whom the recruiter has previously been employed, some may have been recently put into new employment by the same recruiter, while others may have been identified by asking around for names. This business is almost entirely devoted to continually re-approaching these same people on the basis of 'It's about time you changed your job!' The length of service in the present occupation might be two years but could be less, depending on how hungry the 'roll-over' recruiter happens to be at the time. I have known it to be as short as six months! The fact that they may have already taken a fee for putting the candidate into his present job appears to have little effect on their conscience. If the client's only exposure to direct-search recruitment is confined to such practitioners, then it is hardly surprising that they take a cynical stance on the topic.

Let's take what is, I hope, a more objective look at some aspects of the direct-search process purely from the intending employer's point of view. Perhaps you are having real difficulties recruiting salespeople, or even field sales managers. You've tried the agencies, you've advertised, but you just don't seem to be able to generate the kind of candidates you need. So, you consider using the services of a direct-search organization. It is reasonable to assume that any candidates put forward will have comprehensive and direct experience with a track record of sales success, not only with your kind of product, but also within your market-place, i.e. complete salespeople who can get up to speed right away, once they have been introduced to the company's particular products and organization.

There is obviously considerable attraction in this process, for if it is successful, it can produce salespeople from whom a more rapid return can be expected than from those with less direct experience who might emanate from agencies and advertising. It is reasonable to argue that this benefit may be off-set to some degree by the limits of the individual consultant's breadth of industry-knowledge and contact, which is unlikely to embrace as wide a range of potential candidates as national press advertising. However, the quality of the typical candidate is likely to be much higher due to the selective nature of the direct-search process. There is much to be said for the benefits of using the collective skills, knowledge and contacts of the more substantial and well-established direct-search organization, rather than enduring the unavoidable limitations of a lone recruiter, unless his or her skills are very specialized and completely compatible with your product and market-place.

It can also be argued that a job which is not advertised is likely to exclude 'up-and-coming' people who are not yet in the job concerned, but have the talent and qualifications to succeed, and see it as a bigger opportunity and challenge than someone who is already operating in the same capacity. That is true, but in most circumstances employers are seeking proven skills and track-record rather than raw potential. More often than not, users of direct-search services have plenty of internal potential in the process already, but they can't afford the risk (especially the classic of moving their best salesperson into management!) or the time, in prevailing circumstances. They need the assured capability, now.

What about the attitude of the candidate who did not contact you but was approached? There is always a chance that such a recruit may take on the egocentric stance of someone who feels he or she is being pursued, and may feel inclined to dictate the terms. In effect, the employer/employee relationship may get out of phase. For a start, the candidate is likely to expect something special in order to justify the move from a currently successful and satisfactory situation. Higher salary? Better company car? Promise of advancement into management? Profit sharing? Share holding? That could be difficult to justify to your existing sales team. It might even result in the self-defeating situation of departures that could more than off-set the benefit of taking on the new recruit. It is certainly a situation that justifies considerable thought. You have to be sure that the direct-search candidate is prepared to move to your company for a job and rewards that are not significantly out of step with the rest of the organization, and must be moving for the right reasons—career development, better company, better employer, better or more interesting products or market, not exclusively for money.

If a salesperson is prepared to leave a present employer in the lurch 'for a few dollars more', is there any less likelihood that he or she will leave you just as readily as soon as some other company is in need of an instant solution to a transient recruitment problem. Who's to know what this employee's response will be when he or she gets another call from the 'roll-over' recruiter in a few months' time. Loyalty can often be to the detriment of the employee, but when this quality is cancelled out by avarice, it is a dangerous situation for all concerned.

One particular word of warning, and that relates to the use of headhunters, or indeed recruitment consultancies and agencies, in foreign countries. You must bear in mind that it takes a national to find a national. Even if a consultant is fluent in the language of another country, many of the nuances of dialogue and market realities remain unnoticed and unknown. Only those recruitment organizations that are completely conversant with the structure and major players within a particular industry of a given country, as well as completely understanding the terms of employment and rates and methods of payment that apply, can provide an effective recruitment service.

I recall a situation a few years ago where the managing director of a major international company was about to be dismissed. The terrible thing was that I, and many other people in the recruitment business, knew it was going to happen months before he did. This happened because the company, in its wisdom, employed a North American direct-search organization to find a suitable replacement in the UK. The company's apparent belief was that by using a recruitment organization from another country their momentous decision would remain a secret. I am sure the recruiters concerned did the best job they could, but knowing little of the country, the particular industry or any of the individuals within it, they soon ran into problems. By the time they had spoken to a number of likely, but unfortunately inappropriate candidates, the word soon got about, until it appeared that the only person who didn't know about the vacancy was the ousted man himself. Furthermore, several particularly relevant people were overlooked who were obvious contenders to anyone who really knew the local scenario; and the applicant who eventually took the job was unsuccessful. Mistakes were made that few UK recruitment specialists would have allowed to happen due to their knowledge of the market-place.

So much for methodology, opinion and ethical considerations; but what does it typically cost to use the services of a direct-search organization? Well, basic charges can range from 25 per cent to as much as 50 per cent of first-year income, depending on the seniority and importance of the job. Most direct-search organizations in the UK will require staged retainers for an exclusive assignment; typically one-third of the expected fee on assignment, one-third on appointment and one-third on commencement of employment. Though some recruitment organizations operate on a contingency basis, it is more common in the USA than in Europe.

The time scale of a recruitment campaign could last for many months, involving a considerable investment in time and money on the part of the recruiter without any guarantee of success. In addition, the direct-search consultant has to consider the possibility that the right candidates might be located, only to be lost, because the client is unable to persuade the selected person to take the job, even though the agency has completed its part of the recruitment task. Consequently, any demand for partial payment in advance, from a reputable professional recruitment organization providing direct-search services, is normal and justifiable.

Some recruitment companies give either a refund or a free replacement in circumstances where a candidate leaves the job soon after joining. This 'guarantee' period is typically up to three months. In cases where no such refund facility is offered, it is usual that the alternative is a replacement free of charge within a given time period.

For the first few weeks it is difficult for the sales manager to know if the newly acquired salesperson is a good buy or a goodbye. However, it must always be the responsibility of the employer, rather than of the recruitment organization, to make an early judgement on whether or not a new employee is going to make it. On the basis of the truism 'You don't know people until you live with them' one can hardly expect a recruitment agency to give a refund because a new recruit departs after six months' employment.

It is fair to say that not all 'headhunting' is as professional as it might be. It is so easy for those involved to lose sight of the ethical considerations and the best interests of all the parties involved in the process. That includes both those who benefit from the fulfilment of a job vacancy and those who are disadvantaged by the department of an employee. In my experience, it is more likely that lone 'headhunters' who are able to operate without the restriction of corporate guidelines, thorough training and professional practice are the ones most likely to take 'ethical shortcuts'. Certainly, those companies who use direct search cannot complain if it is occasionally directed towards their own employees. 'Those who live by the sword . . .' etc. As far as the direct-search consultant is concerned, he or she must always ask themselves the questions 'Are my actions fair and ethical within the prevailing circumstances?' Sometimes conscience says 'No'. Disregard that at your peril.

What are the broader implications of direct search within the fast-moving and ever-changing high technology environment in which we now exist? Certainly, people change jobs now more frequently than ever before; often too soon to have achieved anything. Simply keeping one step ahead of failure. Therefore, a mechanism for handling this increased traffic of people is unavoidable. Consequently the recruitment industry has grown phenomenally in recent years. There are those who will argue that the recruitment companies are the biggest contributors to a marked decrease in average job-life throughout most industry sectors. Be that as it may, the reality is that the professional recruiter is here to stay, wielding a considerable influence on the fortunes of those organizations whose success is dependent on having the best people at the right time.

Many recruiters will argue that long and loyal service is mostly to the detriment of the individual. They will say that their role is to protect the best interests of working people and enable them to exploit their talents and opportunities to the fullest, in the same way that major corporations are obliged to take whatever actions are necessary to benefit their shareholders the most and guarantee long-term survival. There is obviously an element of self-justification in that stance, but it is not entirely unreasonable.

# 4.

# Details and disciplines

'Skill comes so slow, and life so fast doth fly.'

*Sir John Davies 1569–1626*

## The job specification

Very few sales managers bother to prepare a detailed job specification when they are involved in the recruitment process. Most of them never give the matter a thought. This is particularly surprising in view of the employer's obligations within the Employment Protection Act. The situation is so common that many professional recruitment consultancies provide a standard job specification form for clients wishing to register a job vacancy, because they realize that the chances of being provided with a detailed job description are extremely low. Certainly no independent recruitment organization could possible carry out a recruitment campaign effectively without one!

The job specification is not a piece of bureaucratic nonsense. It makes the sales manager really think about the kind of person needed and tells applicants exactly what is expected of them and what they will receive in return for their labours. There is more to selling than simply 'flogging the product'! Will they be required to complete call reports on a regular basis, limit their activities to a specific area, collect competitive information, work in the evenings, provide a car, swear an oath of allegiance? Candidates need to know what is required of them, as much as the sales manager needs to know the kind of people he or she is seeking.

Some managers are reluctant to produce a job specification because they fear it may be used as evidence against them. On the other hand, it might serve to confirm how unattractive the job actually is. Quite frankly, the sales manager who cannot create a meaningful job specification should not be in management. Surely, by inference, he or she is saying 'I don't know enough about the kind of person I want to hire, or the job, or the tasks I want the new recruit to perform, to be able to put it in writing', or, 'I know what I want, but can't be bothered to document it.' Either reflects very badly upon the efficiency and organizational ability of the sales manager.

Job specifications vary considerably from industry to industry, but within my own company we have evolved the following basic guidelines for sales managers, and for that matter, personnel departments who have sufficient commitment and awareness to do the job properly. The guidelines are designed to cover the basic requirements of both the pre-recruitment situation and the creation of individual terms of employment for new recruits.

### Candidate profile

1. (a) *Experience*
    Amount of experience required or preferred by sales/product/application/industry. Acceptable industry sectors of past/current employment.
    (b) *Academic qualifications*
    'O' Levels/'A' Levels/Degree/Higher Education Certificate, etc.
2. *Preferred age range*
3. *Job title*
4. *Company/Division*
5. (a) *Reporting to*
    Line manager.
    (b) *Functional responsibilities*
    e.g. marketing manager, technical support manager.
6. *Territory*
    e.g. geographic/industry/application.
7. *Location*
    Place from which the salesperson operates, state home if applicable.
8. (a) *Products to be sold*
    Detailed declaration of available product range.
    (b) *Markets*
    Target applications/industries to be addressed.
9. *Revenue objectives*
    Total target within period, by-product/market type as appropriate. What qualifies? Orders, invoices, revenues generated off-territory?
10. *Training to be provided*
    Induction/sales/product/continuing.
11. *Sales support*
    Nature, source, amount, and method of access.
12. *Remuneration*
    Details of compensation plan, including commission, bonus and any over-performance multipliers, clearly stating when payment will be made (on order/invoice/payment/related permutation), together with details of any guaranteed income against commission, declaring how much per month, for how long and clearly stating whether returnable or non-returnable. Also car arrangements, other fringe benefits and entitlements such as pension, health insurance, luncheon vouchers, expense account, relocation arrangements, holidays, share options, etc.

13. *Career path*

    Areas of possible advancement within not only the initial company sector, but also the organization at large.

14. *Job responsibilities*

    Statement of all duties to be performed in the pursuit of sales activity, e.g. pursue profitable sales throughout the defined territory.

    Continually project a professional image of company and self. Always seek the best interests of the company. Maintain a continual new business prospecting process. Sell across the full product range. Maintain and expand existing accounts. Maintain comprehensive client records. Cover the entire sales territory effectively and economically. Produce prompt and pertinent call reports. Attend sales meetings whenever required. Be aware of all competitive activity within the defined territory and report pertinent matters to the sales manager and the marketing department. Ensure all sales aids are kept in good order. Establish credit-worthiness of new clients. Actively pursue overdue accounts. Deal with all client complaints promptly and effectively. Ensure clients fully understand the content and application of any products considered or purchased. Organize client training in the use of products. Pursue self-training on both product and selling. Keep up to date with product and industry developments. Constantly revaluate the importance of clients in accordance with value of established business and new revenue potential, modifying sales activity accordingly. Keep the car provided by the company in clean and roadworthy condition. Complete a full day's work every day. Achieve the company's expected volume of face-to-face sales calls each week. Sell only those products and varieties actually available. Secure prior agreement of management to any non-standard arrangement of product or terms before committing the company to make delivery, etc. etc.

So much for the individual employee's job specification. However, it is not usually necessary to provide this level of detail until the job-offer stage, or even after the commencement of employment. Clearly, it takes a lot of time and effort to obtain this depth of information. Nevertheless, it is important to have a clear statement of the basic details of the job so that the candidate and the interviewer have sufficient understanding of the duties, terms and conditions to be able to discuss the job opportunity and negotiate terms in a well-informed manner. This may appear to be a relatively straightforward matter, but there are so many considerations to bear in mind, that essential details can easily be overlooked.

One way round this problem is to create a form that addresses all the essential points that are likely to be discussed. Though it is unlikely that any such form will be exhaustive, basic information on all the key areas of duty and reward will make it possible for the interviewer, or even a stand-in, to answer most, if not all, of the questions the candidate is likely to ask. It also reduces any risk of misunderstanding between individuals and departments who may be jointly involved in the recruitment process by having 'everyone singing from the same hymn-sheet'! In particular, I am referring to sales directors and sales managers, sales and personnel departments.

Figure 4.1 shows the form we use when gathering basic information for the recruitment of computer industry salespeople. We call it the Job Order form.

## Dealing with applicants

A salesperson answering a recruitment advertisement expects to receive a prompt response. Whether contact is by letter or by telephone—more usually the latter—he or she expects to speak to someone who can qualify the relevance of his or her application and arrange a subsequent interview, if that is appropriate. Any delay is sure to diminish interest.

While failure to respond promptly is most commonly a result of insufficient priority being given to the recruitment process, delay can often be caused by insufficient data being collected from applicants who make contact by telephone. This can create problems, such as having insufficient data to decide on the suitability of a particular applicant, being unable to recontact the candidate because the address or telephone was not noted, or because whatever details were taken have been mislaid, the latter usually being the result of scribbling some information on the nearest scrap of paper, then forgetting about it.

A sensible way of avoiding most of these problems is to create a simple form which contains all the basic personal information you require, such as name, address, home and business telephone numbers, age, qualifications, etc., and details of past employment, including companies, job functions, length of employment, remuneration, products sold, markets, etc. This has several advantages:

Provides greater control of the conversation.
Creates a smoother exchange of information.
Ensures you obtain all the data you need in order to qualify the applicability of the applicant.
Provides a sensible common document for subsequent action.

In my own company we use a variety of such forms from which we can select one which is appropriate for obtaining the right kind of information from whatever kind of applicant happens to call us by telephone. Figure 4.2 is an example of a generic form for gathering telephone information from salespeople. We call it the Candidate Profile form.

Figure 4.3 is a self-explanatory document we use as a master control sheet for response to a particular advertisement. It is kept at the front of the file that contains the telephone application forms and the letters of application received from candidates. It gives the benefit of good control and also provides an instant overview of the quantity and quality of response.

Delay can also be caused by lack of internal co-ordination. It is very important that a specific person is given responsibility for collating all response and

# Job Order

In order to ensure the high professional standards we set at SMR, which above all means sending only relevant candidates to you, we need to ask a lot of essential questions.

| | |
|---|---|
| Originating consultant: | Date: |

| | |
|---|---|
| Company: | Telephone No: |
| Address: | Fax No: |
| | Principal contact: |
| | Title: |

| | |
|---|---|
| Job Title: | When required: |
| Number required: | Location: |
| Sales Area(s): | Size of sales team: |
| | Reporting to: |
| | Title: |

Product(s) to be sold:

Application(s):

Industry/market(s):

Main competitors:

| | |
|---|---|
| Company's Annual Revenue (UK): | Total staff (UK): |
| Size of salesforce (National): | (Local): |

| | |
|---|---|
| Basic salary range: | On-target earnings: |
| Expected first year earnings: | Sales quota—Year 1: |
| Other payments/Bonus: | Sales quota—Year 2: |
| Guarantee and period: | Relocation package: |

**Figure 4.1** Job Order form

## What other benefits?
Company car (Describe)
Health insurance
Pension
Share options
Profit sharing
Promotional opportunities
Job status
Market growth
Company growth
Company reputation
Company stability
Outstanding product performance
High earnings potential
Training
Other

Formal qualifications:                                    Age range:

Required selling experience:

Required product experience:

Required applications experience:

Required industry/market experience:

What are the most important characteristics you are seeking in the right candidate?

## General

What are the three most important duties within the job?

What problems are you trying to solve by hiring this person?

Why is your company a good place to work?

Why should a salesperson who is currently happy and successful, quit his or her job and come to work for you?

What long-term opportunities are associated with this vacancy?

Please send me three copies of your Product Overview and Annual Report

**Figure 4.1**   *(continued)*

## Interviewing

How many interviews will be involved?

Who will carry out the interviews and where?

What will the interviewers focus on? (topics, questions, answers)

Who makes the final decision?

Will psychometric assessment be involved?

## Status of vacancy

How long has this vacancy existed?

Why has it come about?

What recruitment actions have already been taken? (self or external agencies)

How many candidates have been interviewed so far?

What job offers have been made or pending?

**Figure 4.1** *(continued)*

handling telephone calls. It goes without saying that such a person should be totally fluent with every aspect of the job/s concerned, as well as of the company and its products. Obviously, there will be occasions when the designated person is not around, but everyone in the department should know who is handling the particular job vacancy and have an outline understanding of the situation. There is nothing more irritating for a would-be recruit than taking the trouble to make contact with a potential employer only to find that the person they should be speaking to doesn't know much about the job, isn't around at the moment, doesn't call them back; or even worse, nobody seems to know who's dealing with the matter. It gives the impression of being the kind of company they would rather not be working for.

Personnel departments are usually better organized than sales departments for dealing with job applicants. It's the kind of thing they have to deal with most days of the week. Would-be employees are a transient situation for most sales departments, and as a result, the organization to cope with them is usually less efficient than it might be. The most common mistake is to assume that candidates responding by telephone should be handled in much the same way as the incoming mail. You leave your secretary to sort it out and deal with the matter when you can find the time. This obviously introduces the problems of delay that I hope I have sufficiently emphasized already. However, there is another major problem that needs to be considered. Is your secretary able to answer all the questions that are likely to be asked by the candidate, who will want to know about the job responsibilities, the remuneration package, the fringe benefits, the targets, the products, the applications, the markets, and so on. Most secretaries don't have that level of fluency. After all, that isn't their job. However, it is the job of the sales team, so that's who should be providing answers to potential recruits. I'm not suggesting that the whole sales team should be hanging around the office, just in case someone calls; but I am saying that a member of the sales management team or a territory salesperson, who is completely conversant with the jobs involved, should be around during working hours throughout the duration of a self-mounted, advertising-based recruitment campaign.

Clearly, the number of interviews between the first meeting with the candidate and any offer of employment has a significant bearing on the duration of the overall recruitment process. Practice varies considerably from one company to another, but in my opinion it should never take more than two meetings, involving two or more representatives of the employer, to reach a final decision. A good way to hurry the proceedings along, while securing more than one opinion, is to hold 'tandem' interviews. This requires the involvement of two senior people, preferably managers from sales or personnel, with one taking the role of the interviewer and the other acting merely as an observer. It is surprising how much more objective one can be with the help of an immediate second opinion.

On one occasion we had a sales candidate who was invited to attend a third

# Candidate Profile

In order to ensure the high professional standards we set at SMR, which above all means presenting you with relevant job opportunities only, we need to ask you a lot of essential questions.

Originating consultant:                     Date:

Name:                                       Telephone No. (home):

Address:                                    Business:

                                            Car:

                                            Age:

                                            Source of application:

Job required:                               When needed:

Preferred location:                         Relocate?:

**Experience—type and duration**

Selling

Product:

Application(s):

Industry/Market:

**Preferred sales scenario**

Product(s):

Application(s):

Industry (Markets):

What are the main features you are looking for in any new job you might consider?

Present employer:            From:            To:

Job:                         Territory:

Product(s):

Application(s):

Industry/Market(s):

Performance v target this year:     Last year:     Previous year:

Basic salary:                       Sales quota:

On-target earnings:                 Car provided:

Other payments/Bonus:               Fringe benefits (BUPA/Pension)

Projected earnings this year:

**Figure 4.2**  Candidate Profile form

44

| | | |
|---|---|---|
| Previous employer: | From: | To: |
| Job: | Territory: | |
| Product(s): | | |
| Application(s): | | |
| Industry/Market(s): | | |
| Performance v target—last full year: | | |

| | | |
|---|---|---|
| Previous employer: | From: | To: |
| Job: | Territory: | |
| Product(s): | | |
| Application(s): | | |
| Industry/Market(s): | | |
| Performance v target—last full year: | | |

In percentage terms, how committed are you to leaving your present job?

What dissatisfaction do you have with your present situation?

Are there any circumstances that would induce you to stay with your current employer?

What job opportunities are you currently negotiating with other potential employers?

What is the structure of your current remuneration package, and what is the minimum basic salary, on-target earnings and guarantee against commission you will accept?

When are you available for interview?

Please send me your up-to-date c.v.

**Figure 4.2** (*continued*)

# Advertising response

Client............ Journal............ Date............ Ref. No.............

| | Name | Location | Telephone | Interview? | Long list? | Short list? | Job? |
|---|---|---|---|---|---|---|---|
| 1 | | | | | | | |
| 2 | | | | | | | |
| 3 | | | | | | | |
| 4 | | | | | | | |
| 5 | | | | | | | |
| 6 | | | | | | | |
| 7 | | | | | | | |
| 8 | | | | | | | |
| 9 | | | | | | | |
| 10 | | | | | | | |
| 11 | | | | | | | |
| 12 | | | | | | | |
| 13 | | | | | | | |
| 14 | | | | | | | |
| 15 | | | | | | | |
| 16 | | | | | | | |
| 17 | | | | | | | |
| 18 | | | | | | | |
| 19 | | | | | | | |
| Totals | | | | | | | |

Comments

**Figure 4.3** Summary of response to job advertising

interview, which still did not get him beyond the personnel department and in front of the sales manager to whom he would be reporting. He declined the invitation, of course!

Another reason for the failure of sales recruitment is the nature of the interview. Candidates often complain of unsatisfactory meetings, lacking in preparation and devoid of job specification or territory definition. This kind of situation only serves to reduce the credibility of both the manager and the job. It is essential that all interviews are subject to prior preparation with a planned structure to cover all aspects of the job; candidate profile, job specification, company and product description, etc., supported by suitable documentation. After all, the job interview is just another sales situation, but one where both are selling and both are buying. Overcoming objections and final closes are very much part of the action. If the deal feels right, ask for the order!

The initiation of the sales recruitment process must be given considerable thought before it is put into effect. It is very easy for a manager who is already under pressure from his other duties to regard an unexpected demand for new salespeople as an unwanted intrusion and deal with it in a reactive manner, choosing the easiest and most accessible means of recruitment available. For most sales and personnel managers nowadays this means shopping around the recruitment agencies rather that establishing a well-considered strategy tailored to their own particular needs. They believe that the immediate availability of candidates from agency files will speed up the procedure. Very often the reverse is true.

Inevitably, many of the candidates on agency files are available because they have failed in their previous job, or simply shouldn't be in selling at all. Accomplished and inadequate salespeople look much the same on paper; particularly if the agency concerned is not as skilled as it ought to be in its documentation and methods of assessment. A lot of time can be wasted by interviewing unsuitable people in the hope that the right person will turn up eventually. The fact is, outstanding salespeople spend very little time on agency files. They are usually in such short supply that those who do choose to use the services of a recruitment agency are out on interview with established clients before the ink on their application form has dried. Quite apart from that, of all occupational types, salespeople typically have the initiative to identify those companies for whom they would like to work, and make their own arrangements. Yet this reality only makes itself apparent to many sales managers after they have spent many weeks discovering the hard way, via a continuation of fruitless interviews, inadequate candidates and an awful lot of wasted selling time.

I recall a discussion with a client who had previously spent several months of interviewing sales candidates, contributed by a large number of agencies, without any success at all. He had suffered everything from c.v.s that consisted of no more than a single summary page clipped to career details contributed by the candidate, to applicants who had never even met anyone from the agency that was putting them forward. While he appeared to take a philosophical stance about all the time he had wasted seeing people who were almost entirely unsuited to his needs, his frustration was very apparent when he exclaimed, 'I asked them for high-flyers, but all they ever sent me was turkeys!'

## The need for prompt action

Many campaigns for the recruitment of sales personnel result in failure, or significantly fall short of expectation. This is invariably due to the apparent inability of many managers, particularly at branch level, to develop a real sense of urgency in dealing with the process once it has been put into effect. While indecent haste is likely to create the wrong impression, there is no doubt that beyond a period of two to three weeks after initial contact with the candidate, the chances of securing his or her services rapidly decline. In most circumstances the problem is one of establishing the right priorities. Sales managers can easily delude themselves into believing that recruitment should have a lower priority than selling and administration. This may be true for a while, but the passage of time creates its own priorities. It is easy to forget that the delay or neglect of recruitment usually incurs a high premium; particularly in the shape of new-business sales that once deferred are lost forever.

The best kind of respondents to recruitment advertising are very often those who are not actively seeking to change their employment. Their attention may be caught by an advertisement to which they respond, perhaps on impulse, in order to discover more about the job in question. However, once they attend an interview and discover they are a commodity in demand, they are likely to become curious about what other opportunities are available. Any gap in the proceedings provides both the opportunity and incentive to seek alternatives. I have often witnessed the situation where candidates, without having had another job in mind, have replied to an advertisement, and by the time the proceedings have dragged on to the third or fourth interview, they have managed to complete the interview process elsewhere and obtain a firm offer of employment. Ridiculous, but true and recurrent.

## Stay close to the candidate

Gaining the confidence and enthusiasm of a new candidate is not an overnight process; it has to be built with care and consideration, however, the one thing that is most likely to negate all the good work you have done in building up the right kind of relationship, is overt or implied neglect. As I have already stated, no news is bad news from the candidate's point of view. Once he or she has gained the impression that you are disinterested, the chances of success are greatly diminished. It is therefore essential that constant contact with the candidate is maintained throughout the recruitment cycle. The means of communication are obviously not limited to face-to-face meetings. Telephone calls, personal letters, product and company literature through the post, introductions to existing employees, and so on, are all means of letting the candidate know that the matter is still proceeding and that you are enthusiastic about the possibility of making an offer of employment.

If you've got all of this right, and you really believe you're dealing with the kind of salesperson you need for your team, the time comes to make a formal offer of employment, usually both verbally and in writing. That is often when the real problems start, and, contrary to your expectations, you stand the greatest chance of losing the candidate altogether.

Obviously, the candidate will have been giving a lot of thought to the prospect of joining your company, and will have considered the job, the territory, the earnings package, the career development possibilities, and so on; but there is no point in getting excited about the situation, or making any positive plans or commitments until such time as the job is formally offered. As a result, there are many critical events and situations that are likely to be initiated when the sales manager says 'The job is yours. Will you accept it?' It's decision time for the salesperson, and the most critical time in the recruitment cycle. This is when powerful sources of negative influence, that are bent on destroying all the good work you have done so far, come into the reckoning for the very first time. You have become 'the enemy' for competitors you didn't even know you had. Their absolute intention is to ensure that the very last thing the candidate will do is join your company. Which is a bit disconcerting, when you are already planning the role he or she will play in your future, what training will be needed, asking the company secretary to order a company car, and all that stuff.

Consider the following vested interests who are likely to lose if you succeed in recruiting the candidate.

### The family
There is a good chance that the applicant hasn't bothered telling the family about the possibility of moving to a new job. Many will conveniently rationalize the situation by convincing themselves that there is no point in discussing the matter with their partner until there is a definite job on offer. Apart from which, they may perceive the search for re-employment as a statement of failure and don't wish to admit it until such time as the possibility of success can be offered, in the form of an alternative situation.

Whatever the reasons, this could be the moment when all the serious domestic implications are discussed for the very first time. How does the family feel about

- Relocating to another part of the country?
- Moving to new schools?
- Moving from fixed salary to commission?
- Leaving friends and relatives behind?
- Giving up some attractive fringe benefits?

There could well be aspects of the job to which a partner may react negatively and will use every possible persuasion against accepting it. The smart recruiter always tries to ensure that there is domestic support for an offer of employment.

### The present employer

We all know there is a continual shortage of accomplished salespeople, and if they are any good their current employers want to keep them. After all, there are current and prospective revenues to be considered. When a salesperson vacates a territory there is likely to be a significant loss of business; possibly measured in tens of thousands of pounds. Then there is the 'learning curve' that any replacement will unavoidably have to negotiate. Either of these two situations will cost time and money far in excess of the cost of persuading the candidate to stay, perhaps by way of a significant salary increase, a better company car, or even expediting the promotion that his or her current sales manager had been 'seriously considering for quite a long time'. It is very much in the interests of any sales manager to use every possible means to retain the services of a successful and respected salesperson.

### Other potential employers

Applicants may profess to be interested in no other job opportunity but yours. Sadly, many job applicants tell lies! They don't mean to of course, it's just the way things work out. Their assessment of the situation is that you are likely to take less interest in them if you realize they are also applying their enthusiasm to your competitors. So, they rationalize the situation on the basis of 'what you don't know you won't worry about'.

More often than not candidate salespeople will be 'playing the market' for the best deal they can get; but that's to be expected. After all, you are dealing with salespeople and it is in their very nature to negotiate the best deal. So, it is wise to always work on the assumption that, irrespective of what the candidate says, you are competing with 'the enemy' for the candidate's services. In other words, it is best to treat the matter of closing the sale with the candidate, as seriously as you would any other direct selling confrontation with your main competitors.

### Recruitment organizations

The instinctive reaction of most recruitment consultants, on hearing the news that the candidate has accepted employment, or is about to do so, with some organization other than one of those to which they have sent him, is not to offer their congratulations. They are more likely to launch into a well-considered presentation of reasons why such a decision would not be in the candidate's best interests. After all, that is the job of recruitment consultants. They are much better qualified and better practised than you are to come up with plausible reasons why one job is better than another. Their income depends on it, and so does yours; which means you have temporarily to consider all recruitment agencies also, other than the one who has provided your applicant, to be direct competitors.

And just when you thought you'd solved your recruitment problem!

## The 'on-target earnings' trap

In most industries, a significant proportion of the salesperson's income is derived from commission earnings. Indeed, one could say that the biggest difference between salespeople and other working people is that, for the greater part, their income is dependent on personal success. Some companies pay salary only, but this tends to be the exception rather than the rule. In some situations the salesperson's income is entirely dependent on commission.

Consequently, it can often be very difficult for either the employer or potential employee (or even an existing salesperson at the beginning of a new sales year!) to determine what they are likely to earn. There are so many factors that can affect the salesperson's performance, beyond the basic question of the ability to sell. The presence or absence of product promotion (advertising, press relations, etc.) clearly has a bearing on sales, as do economic fluctuations, production capacity, availability of raw materials, etc. etc. Consequently, the salesperson's income is not entirely a function of his or her own endeavours. Yet, over and above that, other factors have to be considered very closely; especially by new recruits.

1. 'How long will it take to receive all relevant training in order to achieve product fluency and go out and sell effectively?'

2. 'How long will it take to thoroughly quantify the new business potential of my sales territory?'

3. 'How long is the duration of the selling-cycle?' (The typical length of time from initial contact to the closing of the sale.)

4. 'Irrespective of external factors, how much business can reasonably be generated by this product, in this territory within this market-place?'

These are very important questions because they all have a direct bearing on how much the salesperson can realistically expect to earn within a given timescale.

Sadly, few sales managers go through this kind of evaluative process. Consequently, their contribution to the topic of potential earnings is often limited to generalities and sweeping statements.

The most common and misleading of these is the term 'on-target earnings'. This is a declaration of the total amount of income that will be earned on achieving 100 per cent of the stated sales objective. It is calculated by setting the appropriate rate/s of commission, plus any additional payments and bonuses, against the annual sales target and adding the basic salary. Of course, this process works on the assumption that the sales target is reasonable; and more importantly, that it is also achievable.

Salespeople change jobs for a variety of reasons:

1. To broaden their experience in terms of product, market or job function.

2. To get away from an unsatisfactory situation, in company, product or management terms.

3.   To escape from an unhappy personal relationship.

4.   To secure a particularly attractive external job opportunity.

5.   To increase personal status or challenge.

. . . and so on.

Few salespeople decide to seek a new employer simply for higher rewards; there has to be an accompanying motivation that swings the balance in that direction. They may move because of failure or because the difficulty of achieving current sales objectives is having an adverse effect on their ability to earn; but they do not put themselves on the job market in order to earn a few hundred, or even a few thousand, pounds more on achieving target. What's the point, especially after tax? At least they know the reality of their present situation, and whether or not the current sales objectives and potential earnings are realistic. There are no such guarantees as far as a new employer is concerned. Furthermore, there is the pain and frustration of giving up all those hard-won prospects and personal contacts and starting all over again with an unfamiliar product, company, territory, etc. Not a very attractive proposition.

However, when it is necessary for a salesperson to make a voluntary or compulsory decision to take his or her talents elsewhere, money is obviously a significant aspect of the negotiations. It is in this situation that the salesperson is vulnerable to the 'on-target earnings' trap, and the would-be employer can lose a good candidate, simply because a true statement of the facts does not compare favourably with some other company's wishful thinking, as far as potential earnings is concerned.

The key word is *achievable*!

1.   Can the task that has been set actually be accomplished?

2.   Is the product competitive enough in terms of price and performance?

3.   Is there actually a proven and substantial market for it?

4.   Has the territory concerned been nurtured and developed, or has it been 'raped and pillaged' by the previous incumbent?

5.   Has the company got the financial clout and the production capability to deliver and support its products in a satisfactory manner?

6.   Does the sales target make sense in terms of what comparable companies are asking of their salespeople in similar circumstances?

7.   Is a substantial proportion of the existing sales force already earning at the stated level?

Such input is obviously very important but it is insufficient to leave the qualifications of the sales target to such broad comparisons; more detail is essential.

The first test is to consider how the sales target for the territory concerned is actually calculated. You would be surprised how naive the process can be within many companies. Is it merely the national target divided by the number of people in the sales force? That's great news for the salesperson in central London but what about the one in north Wales? It is important to ensure that any sales target is customized to the territory concerned, accounting for its unique problems and opportunities and the implications of the inevitable 'learning curve' that any new employee must experience. To have the same target as other established salespeople could be a nonsense in many circumstances.

Another method of checking a target is to break it down into the number of face-to-face sales calls per day and the amount of prospecting activity that can be expected in order to achieve the stated sales objectives.

1. What is the value of a typical sale?

2. How many sales need to be made in a year in order to achieve quota?

3. How many qualified prospects (as opposed to 'suspects'!) need to be generated in order to produce the number of sales required, assuming the typical ratio of conversion from prospects to sales?

4. How many sales calls and/or demonstrations does this imply?

5. How much prospecting, by way of letter writing, telephoning, cold canvassing, etc. will be necessary to set up the required number of sales calls and demonstrations?

6. How much time is likely to be taken up by travelling around the designated territory?

7. How much time is likely to be taken up by sales meetings and general administration?

If the result of such calculations is an apparent demand for a ten-day-week, then there is obviously something wrong with the sales target, to say little of the manager who set it!

I recall a situation a few years ago when a client, to whom I had sent an excellent candidate for a selling job, bitterly complained to me because the applicant had been lost to one of his competitors. He believed the remuneration package offered by his company was very reasonable. It was based on realistic objectives and provided total earnings above average for the industry. The territory was a good one and the company's product was excellent. Yet the potential recruit went to work for a competitor, simply because he could earn some £5000 per annum more on achievement of quota. However, it transpired that the sales target set by the competitor was almost twice as big as the one our client had proposed. Furthermore, if the salesman had been able to achieve with our client the total sales required by the competitor, he would actually have earned some £10 000 above quota, i.e. £5000 more than with the company he decided to join!

Maybe the candidate decided against our client for reasons other than financial implications, but it is almost certain he fell into the 'on-target earnings' trap, simply by not working out what could be earned as an employee with either company for a given revenue figure, as opposed to the achievement of sales target.

# 5.

# *Assessment and selection*

---

'God does not play dice.'

*Albert Einstein 1879–1955*

## The salesperson's point of view

As in any selling situation (for that is the context in which recruitment should be viewed) it is important to understand the rationale of the buyer, i.e. the potential recruit. This is best achieved by first considering how a salesperson is likely to go about finding a new job.

The first step is to decide where the best job opportunities are most likely to occur. Advertisements are an obvious source. Sunday and daily newspapers, trade journals, or even commercial radio, are all prospective sources of job announcements. There are also recruitment organizations providing a variety of services for locating jobs. All that has to be done is to select the means most suited to his or her particular requirements. Unfortunately, this is not as easy as it might appear. Let us first of all consider the kind of questions likely to be asked by a well-informed salesperson who has decided to seek alternative employment.

1.  'What sort of job, with which type of company, will improve my curriculum vitae the most? i.e. Will the job I am considering enhance my market value?'

2.  'Can I be absolutely confident that the company I am considering will stay in business for the foreseeable future? Is it financially stable and is it making adequate investment into new products?'

3.  'Are the sales targets really achievable?'

4.  'What is the real income potential with what guarantees in the first full year of employment, based on the actual earnings of existing salespeople?'

5.  'What are the real prospects for career advancement, and what is the record of promotion among the present sales force over the past five years?'

6.  'What training will I need in order to succeed in this job, and how does this requirement compare with the training my prospective employer is planning to provide?'

7. 'How will my personal income be affected by giving up the prospect portfolio generated in my current job?'

8. 'To what degree will the financial benefits of the job I am considering be negated by the direct and indirect costs and inconvenience of relocation, travel, housing, etc., and any increase in everyday living costs applicable to the location in question?'

9. 'Are the responsibilities of the job accompanied by appropriate authority?'

10. 'Am I convinced that the product I shall be expected to sell can command my absolute belief and conviction?'

11. 'Could I work happily and effectively with the person who is to be my direct superior?' (This is probably the most crucial question of all!)

There is, of course, another important set of questions the candidate is likely to be asking before starting to look around, and certainly before finally accepting a new job: Have I really exhausted the opportunities with my present employer? What is my established income really worth compared with the unproven potential of a new job? Have I really completed the job I set out to do? Perhaps no potential employer has given me a good enough justification for turning my back on the 'devil I know'. That is often the case when an intending employer fails to sell the company and the job opportunity in a positive and enthusiastic manner.

## The application form

Some companies have the advantage of employing a personnel manager who has a good understanding of salespeople. Such a person is likely to be better equipped than the sales manager for sorting out the initial response to a recruitment campaign, more able to identify the valid applicants, the time-wasters, the 'guarantee-hoppers' and those who should never have applied in the first place. To the last three categories of applicants the personnel manager is likely to send a standard letter—Thanks, but no thanks! The others will probably receive an application form.

This is where the role of the sales manager begins. Don't let the personnel department simply send out that tired old application form. Why not augment it with a single sheet containing questions that make a real contribution to the selection process as far as salespeople are concerned?

1. 'How long have you been selling?'

2. 'How long have you been selling our kind of products in our market-place?'

3. 'What formal sales and product training have you received?'

4. 'What has been your achievement against sales targets over the past five years?'

5. 'Who are your main competitors?'

6. 'Provide names of some companies to whom you have made notable sales in the past two years.'

7. 'What kind of job are you really looking for?'

   . . . and so on.

This will give you a much enhanced perception of the individual applicant, and provides some interesting points of discussion for the interview.

   Having decided upon those you want to see, there are some important considerations to be made before the first applicants start to get their interview suits pressed.

   First of all, if you haven't created a job specification yet, now is the time to do so (see Chapter 4). You can't expect an applicant to get enthusiastic about working for a sales manager who doesn't have detailed knowledge of the job. Candidates will expect to have precise details about territory boundaries, remuneration, targets, training, company transport, job title, existing clients, relocation, competition, fringe benefits, and so on. It is not only time saving and constructive but also gives a good impression when you are able to say to a candidate, 'This is what the job is about—do you think you qualify and are you interested?'

   Figure 5.1 is a sample of the application form we use in my own company for recruiting sales and sales support people within the computer industry. Note the collection of direct references, performance against target and names of competitors in part (b) and the demand for selling, product, applications and market information in part (c). This is invaluable information for creating the initial 'long-list' and provides useful input for the interview iteself.

## The interview

Many interviews take the form of a friendly chat where any topic more relevant than the state of the weather is purely incidental. Maybe that's a slight exaggeration, but certainly a large proportion of sales managers do not pre-plan their interviews. Their 'preparation' for the meeting only begins when their secretary announces the arrival of the aspiring candidate. That doesn't do a lot for effective evaluation of the applicant or for the credibility of the sales manager in the eyes of the potential recruit. Yet, this kind of situation can easily be overcome by the creation of a formal structure within which the essential substance of the interview is contained. We have developed a series of structured interviews within my own company, each consisting of five elements:

1. The company.

2. The job.

Sales and Marketing Services Group

# Sales & Marketing Recruiters Ltd

*London Office:*
29 Oxford Street, London W1R 1RE
Telephone: 01 746 2213

*Midlands Office:*
Sales & Marketing House, Beacon Street, Lichfield, Staffs. WS13 7AA
Telephone: 0543 414040   Fax: 0543 256024

## APPLICATION FOR PROFESSIONAL EMPLOYMENT

### PERSONAL DETAILS

| | | | | | | |
|---|---|---|---|---|---|---|
| Full Name | | | | | Date of application | |
| Home Address | | | | | Own Home? | For How Long? |
| | | | | | Home Telephone No. | |
| Age | Weight | Height | Own Car? | Would you Relocate? | Preferred Location | |
| Marital Status | | No. of Children | | Advert Reference No. | Current Driving Licence | |
| Nationality | | Date of Birth | | Any recent illness? | Any physical disability? | |
| When available for interview? | | How were you introduced to SMR? | | Salary Required: Least considered: | | |
| Hobbies, Sports, etc. | | | | Have you ever been declared bankrupt? | | |
| Describe any outside business interests | | | | | | |
| To what professional or business organisation(s) do you belong? | | | | | | |

### EDUCATIONAL DETAILS

| | NAME | From | To | SUBJECTS | ACHIEVEMENTS |
|---|---|---|---|---|---|
| SECONDARY | | | | | |
| COLLEGE OR UNIVERSITY | | | | | |
| OTHER | | | | | |
| PROFESSIONAL QUALIFICATIONS: | | | | | |

| LANGUAGES | Read | Write | Speak | FLUENT? | | Technical | Social |
|---|---|---|---|---|---|---|---|
| | | | | Yes | No | | |
| | | | | | | | |
| | | | | | | | |
| | | | | | | | |

**Figure 5.1**   Recruitment consultancy's job application form (computer industry)

**EMPLOYMENT HISTORY**

| DETAILS | PRESENT/LAST JOB | | PREVIOUS JOB | | 2nd PREVIOUS JOB | | 3rd PREVIOUS JOB | |
|---|---|---|---|---|---|---|---|---|
| COMPANY NAME | | | | | | | | |
| TELEPHONE No. | | | | | | | | |
| DATES EMPLOYED | From | To | From | To | From | To | From | To: |
| JOB TITLE | | | | | | | | |
| GEOGRAPHIC RESPONSIBILITY | | | | | | | | |
| No. OF PEOPLE YOU SUPERVISE(D) | | | | | | | | |
| YOUR DIRECT SUPERIOR | Name Title | | Name Title | | Name Title | | Name Title | |
| ANNUAL REMUNERATION | SALARY COMMISSION BONUS | | SALARY COMMISSION BONUS | | SALARY COMMISSION BONUS | | SALARY COMMISSION BONUS | |
| DESCRIBE YOUR JOB FUNCTION AND RESPONSIBILITIES (include Product(s) sold - where applicable) | | | | | | | | |
| % PERFORMANCE AGAINST TARGET LAST FOUR YEARS | Last 3. | 2 4 | Last 3. | 2 4 | Last 3. | 2 4 | Last 3. | 2 4 |
| NOTABLE ACHIEVEMENTS | | | | | | | | |
| REASON FOR LEAVING | | | | | | | | |
| NOTICE REQUIRED | | | | | | | | |
| NAME TWO OF YOUR COMPANY'S MAIN COMPETITORS | 1. 2. | | 1. 2. | | 1. 2. | | 1. 2. | |

**Figure 5.1** *(continued)*

## SALES AND MARKETING EXPERIENCE

| How many years experience of sales and marketing do you have? | | |
|---|---|---|
| | Territory Sales ( ) | Sales Management ( ) |
| | Marketing ( ) | Marketing Management ( ) |

| What is the prime product of your present employer? | Into which markets are you selling? |
|---|---|
| **Which aspects of selling/management do you like most?** | **Which aspects of selling/management do you like least?** |

| In which areas of computing do you have significant selling experience? | | | | | |
|---|---|---|---|---|---|
| | Turnkey Systems — Commercial ( ) | CAD/CAM and Graphics ( ) | Microcomputers (End-User) ( ) | Computer Leasing ( ) |
| | Services — Commercial ( ) | Communications Equipment ( ) | Microcomputers (Dealer) ( ) | Maintenance Services ( ) |
| | Services — Technical ( ) | Office Automation ( ) | Peripherals (End-User) ( ) | Training Services ( ) |
| | Applications Software ( ) | Mainframe (Manufacture) ( ) | Peripherals (OEM) ( ) | Management ( ) |
| | Systems Software ( ) | Minicomputers (Manufacture) ( ) | Computer Supplies ( ) | Systems House/Consultancy ( ) |

| State number of years direct selling experience by computer type. | | | | | |
|---|---|---|---|---|---|
| | CDC ( ) | ICL ( ) | BRGHS. ( ) | H.P. ( ) | ( ) |
| | DEC ( ) | NCR ( ) | D.G. ( ) | SPERRY ( ) | ( ) |
| | IBM ( ) | PRIME ( ) | HONEY. ( ) | ( ) | ( ) |

## APPLICATIONS EXPERIENCE
(Indicate years of experience, including any additional items.)

| | | | | |
|---|---|---|---|---|
| Commercial Acctng. ( ) | Database ( ) | Retailing ( ) | Engineering ( ) | Graphics ( ) |
| Stock Control ( ) | Financial Managmt. ( ) | Loc. Governmt. ( ) | Scientific ( ) | Artificial Int. ( ) |
| Manufacturing ( ) | Managmt. Inf. Syst. ( ) | Prog. Conversion ( ) | Office Automation ( ) | Compiler Design ( ) |
| CAD/CAM ( ) | Personnel ( ) | ( ) | ( ) | ( ) |
| ( ) | ( ) | ( ) | ( ) | ( ) |
| ( ) | ( ) | ( ) | ( ) | ( ) |
| ( ) | ( ) | ( ) | ( ) | ( ) |
| ( ) | ( ) | ( ) | ( ) | ( ) |
| ( ) | ( ) | ( ) | ( ) | ( ) |

## COMPUTING EXPERIENCE
(Indicate years of experience, including any additional items.)

| JOB | | COMPUTERS (State model) | | OPERATING SYSTEMS | | LANGUAGES | | SOFTWARE TOOLS | |
|---|---|---|---|---|---|---|---|---|---|
| Operations | ( ) | IBM | ( ) | DOS/VS VSE | ( ) | Cobol | ( ) | CICS | ( ) |
| Programming | ( ) | AMDAHL | ( ) | OS/VSI | ( ) | Assembler | ( ) | IMS | ( ) |
| Systems Analysis | ( ) | ICL | ( ) | MVS | ( ) | Basic | ( ) | IDMS | ( ) |
| Systems Design | ( ) | UNISYS | ( ) | VMEB | ( ) | RPG | ( ) | DMS | ( ) |
| Project Control | ( ) | DEC | ( ) | ME 29 | ( ) | PLAN | ( ) | CMS | ( ) |
| Technical Support | ( ) | HEWLETT PACKARD | ( ) | OS 1100 | ( ) | PL I | ( ) | DATABASE | ( ) |
| D.P. Management | ( ) | BULL | ( ) | GCOS | ( ) | ADA | ( ) | VTAM | ( ) |
| Consultancy | ( ) | DATA GENERAL | ( ) | UNIX | ( ) | FORTRAN | ( ) | VSAM | ( ) |
| Pre-Sales Support | ( ) | PRIME | ( ) | XENIX | ( ) | PASCAL | ( ) | TOTAL | ( ) |
| Post-Sales Support | ( ) | TANDEM | ( ) | JCL | ( ) | APL | ( ) | FILETAB | ( ) |
| O & M | ( ) | ALTOS | ( ) | CP/M (MP/M) | ( ) | ALGOL | ( ) | SHADOW | ( ) |
| Technical Author | ( ) | M.D.I.S. | ( ) | MS-DOS | ( ) | CORAL | ( ) | TDS | ( ) |
| | ( ) | PYRAMID | ( ) | PC-DOS | ( ) | C | ( ) | TDP | ( ) |
| | ( ) | MOTOROLA | ( ) | ( ) | | ( ) | | ( ) | |
| | ( ) | | ( ) | ( ) | | ( ) | | ( ) | |
| | ( ) | | ( ) | ( ) | | ( ) | | ( ) | |
| | ( ) | | ( ) | ( ) | | ( ) | | ( ) | |
| | ( ) | | ( ) | ( ) | | ( ) | | ( ) | |

**Figure 5.1** *(continued)*

**ADDITIONAL INFORMATION**

| What is the nature of any dissatisfaction you may have with your present employer? |
|---|
|  |

| What kind of job are you seeking? |
|---|
|  |

| What fringe benefits do you get from your present job? (Company car, health insurance, pension, share options, etc?) |
|---|
|  |

Please quote two relevant references:

| NAME | OCCUPATION | COMPANY | ADDRESS | TELEPHONE |
|---|---|---|---|---|
|  |  |  |  |  |

| If there is any further information you would like to provide related to your present job, career aspirations, etc., please do so here |
|---|
|  |

**Figure 5.1** (*continued*)

3. Key questions.

4. Career history.

5. Conclusions.

First of all it is important that candidates get a good appreciation of the kind of company they are considering. If they are going to invest their future with a new employer, they need to be confident that they've chosen the right one.

This can be achieved by preparing a concise presentation to be given to every applicant as a preliminary to the interview proper. Some of our clients have gone to the trouble of producing a company video for the express purpose of selling the company to new recruits. Salespeople in particular need to know about the company's products, applications, markets, revenues, profits, growth, research and development, and all those other good things that make them want to go out and invest their career and future wellbeing into your products. Above all, they need to be sold to with all the enthusiasm the company would expect of them. Sitting back with your feet on the desk, expecting applicants to persuade you to offer them a job is a 'one-way street' that seldom works to good effect.

Then there is the job. The candidates need to know about the responsibilities and rewards, the lines of reporting and internal communications, the territory, the particular product they will be selling, and so on. You can't expect them to be positive about the job if they aren't completely sure what it is. The best way of ensuring that all the necessary information can be provided is to ensure a job specification is available at the interview. (See 'The job specification,' Chapter 4.)

Nevertheless, some measure of the candidates' initiative and enthusiasm for the job is whether or not they have gone to the trouble of discovering something about your company and its business for themselves. After all, it doesn't make a lot of sense to take the time out for a job interview if the company and its product arena are not compatible with one's personal aspirations. High-calibre candidates would no more attend an interview without having researched the company than they would make a sales call without pre-call preparation—if you see my point.

Every interview should contain well-considered questions that focus on the basic qualities that are essential in the right person for the job. They could relate to personal background, qualifications, experience, sales performance, and so on. If such a source of essential information is merely committed to memory, the chances are that most of the questions will never be asked, temporarily driven from the mind by the rigours of the interview. There is a simple and obvious way of avoiding that problem. Put them down on paper in a form that enables a summary of the candidate's responses to be noted. That way, you ask all the questions and remember all the answers.

In my own company we use a series of generic forms for this purpose, which we tend to modify according to the requirements of each job. Figure 5.2 shows part of a document we use for recruiting experienced salespeople.

The next element of the structured interview is the career history. While this may appear to be a straightforward sequential exercise there is a grave danger that, if the interviewer does not take the right approach, the kind of information one will obtain will be just like the typical curriculum vitae one tends to receive from job applicants, i.e. a list of job titles, duties, applications, markets, products, etc., but little or nothing about the most important aspect of a salesperson's credentials. 'What did you actually achieve?'

There is very little value to be gained from a company-by-company discourse on job responsibilities, though it may give some idea of career development. What the interviewer needs to know is 'How successful a salesperson are you, and how relevant are your achievements to our requirements?' This is best achieved by moving through the annual selling-cycle and asking, year by year, 'What were you selling? What was your performance against sales target? Give me some examples of your most notable successes in that year.'

Clearly, sales achievements beyond the last five years tend to be less relevant than more recent victories. After all, the best candidates will have current experience that is relevant to your present needs. So, concentrate on today's realities rather than past glories.

By the way, beware of applicants who can't remember what their targets were over the past two or three years and how they actually performed against them. You won't find many successful salespeople who don't know exactly what their recent sales achievements were down to the detail of the actual buyer's names. Those salespeople who don't recall their precise sales accomplishments over the past few years have usually forgotten because it is convenient to do so, or they simply don't wish to remember.

Eventually, the interview comes to a close, and if it's taken more than an hour, or at least an hour and a quarter, then you need to tighten up your control of the interview.

This is the time for making decisions. In my experience, if you don't feel comfortable with the applicant now, you never will. So, have the confidence to let the candidate know your reactions there and then. It's not always easy. Sometimes you're just not sure. My advice? When in doubt, don't!

If you want to offer the candidate a job or move on to the next stage of appraisal, then be sure you give all the enthusiasm you've got. Describe the present attractions of the job and its futures as well. Let the applicant know that both career and rewards will be enhanced by joining your company, and above all make it clear that you believe you could get on well together. That's the most important thing. No rewards can compensate for an unsatisfactory working relationship.

Anyone whom you decide is not the employee for you should be let down with their confidence still intact, strengths reaffirmed, believing that failure to get the job was marginal and perhaps in competition with lots of other better qualified applicants. Wish them good luck in their quest for the right job and bid them goodbye. It doesn't cost anything, and caring makes everyone feel better. Besides which, one day it might be you!

# Interview analysis—experienced salespeople

Name of candidate:          Date:

1.  What personal qualities have brought about the success in your career to date?

2.  How would you describe your style of selling?

3.  What is your strongest selling skill?

4.  What is your weakest selling skill?

5.  What has been your performance against sales targets over the past four years?

6.  What circumstances have caused less than 100% performance?

7.  What recent success demonstrates your ability as an accomplished sales professional?

8.  How many face-to-face sales calls do you make in a typical week?

9.  How many clients and/or 'hot' prospects are you handling at the present time?
    Existing clients:

    'Hot' prospects:

**Figure 5.2**   Interview analysis form for experienced applicants

10. What is the extent of your experience related to our particular product, applications and the industries we serve?

11. What is the typical length of your selling-cycle from first contact to 'close'?

12. What aspect of our company, and this job in particular, interests you the most?

13. What are the main contributions you believe you could make to the success of this company?

14. Where would you like the next two steps in your career to take you?

15. What do you need in order to get real satisfaction from your next job?

16.* What dissatisfaction do you have with your present situation?

17.* Are there any circumstances that would induce you to stay with your current employer?

18.* What other job opportunities are you currently negotiating with other potential employers?

19.* What is the structure of your current remuneration package, and what is minimum basic salary, on-target earnings and guarantee against commission you will accept?

20. Can you give me the names of two pertinent referees who could verify your sales record?

* *These questions may already be answered on the Candidate Profile form.*

**Figure 5.2** (*continued*)

This is a fairly obvious segmentation of the interviewing process in a predictable yet modifiable sequence, but it achieves a number of necessary objectives:

1.  The candidate gets to know everything about the job.

2.  The interviewer gets to know everything about the candidate.

3.  The interviewer controls the interview.

4.  The structure makes it easy to keep the dialogue relevant and the duration of the interview predictable.

5.  It is easy to terminate the interview prematurely on the completion of one of the discrete elements if circumstances demand it.

Certainly, in my own company we could not thoroughly evaluate our candidates while maximizing our use of time without it. I am sure a similar approach is crucial for any sales manager who wishes to utilize interviewing time effectively. The structure need not be the same, but there has to be a planned format to ensure that interviewer and candidate get to know all they wish to know about each other. Furthermore, it must ensure that the company, the product and the job are 'sold' effectively to the potential employee.

So much for the shape of the interview; but that is merely the foundation on which the process of evaluation is built. Let's augment this with some basic guidelines for ensuring that you have the best possible chance of getting it right.

1.  Be well prepared. Know the job, know the product, know the organization. From the candidate's point of view, the main purpose of the meeting is to find out everything about the job and then persuade you into making a job-offer. If it isn't clear what the job is all about, it won't be worth asking for, so the interviewee will only be following his of her instincts as a salesperson, without any intention of pursuing the matter further.

    Have your questions ready, and be ready for the questions.

2.  Don't forget the interview is a two-way sell. Don't simply sit there expecting the visitor to 'zap' it to you. You are supposed to explain why the applicant should invest his or her talents with your company.

3.  For goodness' sake, reference-check *every* applicant before making the final offer. If you can do so independently, so much the better. Candidates often bend the truth and so do referees. It is easy to produce a reference by dwelling on the saving graces and carefully avoiding the obvious weaknesses. Most people instinctively want to say nice things about other people, even if it hurts like hell to do so. Consequently, it is essential that past employers are asked pertinent questions likely to provide an insight to the truth.

(a) What are the candidate's strengths?

(b) What are his weaknesses?

(c) How did he perform against target?

(d) What did customers think of him?

(e) Did he always put the hours in?

(f) Was he a good 'opener' and 'closer'?

(g) How did he get along with his colleagues?

(h) Is he absolutely trustworthy?

(i) What was his biggest achievement for your company?

(j) Where you disappointed to lose him?

. . . and so on.

(By the way, bearing in mind that lies demand more consideration than truth, be on your guard for answers that are hesitant.)

4. Get a second opinion on the candidate from one of your colleagues, either by involving them in the interview or getting them to do so separately. This gives a much more objective view of the situation. It's amazing how objective one can be about a candidate by simply sitting on the sidelines as a passive observer while someone else carries out the actual interview. A discipline I regularly exercise in my own recruitment business is to ask our receptionist or one of the secretaries for their opinion of a candidate, based on the appearance and behaviour of the individual concerned in the reception area. Despite such limited exposure, they are invariably right.

5. Avoid limiting your search to the ideal candidate, particularly in the form of your own image. It is so easy to fall into the trap of expecting all good salespeople to look and act like clones of yourself. Getting other people involved with the interview helps to avoid this subjective problem.

6. Be sure to take personal presentation into account, but don't rely on physical appearance. Certainly candidates with dirty fingernails, crumpled clothes, grubby shoes or otherwise unkept appearance are unlikely to be suitable material. After all, this must be the way they intend to present themselves to your clients. On the other hand, don't be put off by plain features, unusual stature, or a heavy regional accent. Concentrate on the candidate's eyes, conduct, ability to communicate easily and positively, sincerity, knowledge, commitment and how comfortable you feel to be with him or her. That's what will be important to your clients, so it must be important to you.

7. Don't oversell the job, tell it like it is, warts and all. Don't augment the job with fantasy and wishful thinking just because you have an excellent candidate in front of you. By all means emphasize the good points, but don't exaggerate them and don't pretend you don't have problems when you know they may have a real effect on the success or failure of the candidate who joins your company. Overstating the achievements and opportunities can only result in subsequent discontent.

8.  Be on the lookout for 'tips of icebergs'; small points that may imply big problems:

    (a) Has the candidate had too many jobs? In other words, did those past jobs last long enough to complete the task originally set? Many candidates have the knack of keeping one step ahead of failure. If past jobs have been short-lived, the chances are the same will apply here.

    (b) What progress has been made over the years in terms of sales achievement, breadth of knowledge and level of responsibility? You need to avoid those candidates who have consistently fallen short of their sales objectives or whose responsibilities have been eroded without good reason.

    (c) Get to know the candidate's domestic situation. Can it interfere with the job? What support is likely to come from home? Is he or she happy? A settled and supportive domestic situation can make an immense contribution to the success of the individual salesperson.

    (d) Is the candidate intelligent enough to handle the job or conversely, so brainy as to find the product and the market boring? A good match is most important. If the product is technical, then a numerate mind is likely to be essential, possibly with appropriate academic qualifications. If the salesperson finds the product unstimulating and undemanding the changes are he or she will become demotivated and eventually walk away from the job.

    (e) Has the candidate had substantial periods of self-employment? If so, maybe this job is a stop-gap to 'keep the wolf from the door'. Once the market recovers or the creditors are paid off, self-determination may prove too much of an attraction.

    (f) And what about loyalty? In other words, does the would-be employee make derogatory remarks about his or her existing company, products, boss, etc. If so, beware! It is not possible to build a sustained and trusting relationship with someone who lacks loyalty and integrity.

Of course, there are always other factors to consider that are unique to a particular job situation. The most important of all is simply taking the time to consider what you are really looking for and what the job actually is. This demands an interviewing process that enables you to discover the truth about the candidate and present him or her with the realities of your company and your product. Selecting people to suit your own situation is an enormously difficult task, where getting it right even half of the time is a considerable accomplishment. One only has to consider the frequency of divorce to see how often the people-matching process fails.

An old friend of mine has a people-evaluation process he calls the 'Trenches Test'. After some exposure to the person concerned, having satisfied himself about their basic credentials, he says to himself 'How happy would I have been, bogged down in the trenches of the First World War, knowing this man was my only companion and support?' He believes it focuses his mind on the 'bottom line' of human relationship.

## Basic considerations of candidate evaluation

As I have already explained, the main purposes of the structured interview are to ensure that all the essential elements of the interview actually occur and that the interviewer sustains control over the proceedings. This does not necessarily imply that it will automatically provide a clear insight to the nature of the applicant. Consequently, it is essential that the interviewer also defines some positive objectives in terms of the candidate's human characteristics and qualifications.

### 1. Presentation

What is the first impression you have of the candidate? Remember, this is the impression likely to be given to your clients. Do you feel comfortable at the prospect of this person representing your company?

What about his or her dress? What kind of person does it imply? Tidy and well organized or scruffy and undisciplined? It matters! It's all about credibility and that Nixonian question, 'Would I buy a used car from this person?'

What about deportment? A stoop and a slouch or erect and brisk? Don't kid yourself that physical appearance has no bearing on mental attitudes; quite the contrary. If an individual cares, is enthusiastic, confident and aware, it shows in the way that they carry themselves. It's a bit like the Oxford and Cambridge boat race. You don't have to watch the race to know who the winners are. All you need is a picture of the crews immediately after the race, and see the slumped and rounded shoulders of the losers.

The ability to communicate fluently is obviously an essential quality for successful salespeople. How easily do they put their story across, steer the conversation to their best advantage? Do they listen carefully and make points clearly and concisely? Are they easy to understand, with a voice that lies comfortably on the ear? What overall impression of their communication skills do you receive? These may appear to be highly subjective questions, but they are the same questions your customers will be asking themselves. A salesperson needs to be enthusiastic, empathetic, knowledgeable and self-assured, giving an impression of the kind of person you could trust and would enjoy having around? Remember the 'Trenches Test'?

### 2. Achievements

The most common failing in personal career histories generated by job applicants is that they concentrate on what they have been doing as opposed to what they have actually achieved. It is all very interesting to discover that a salesperson was responsible for a past employer's most important customers and that the company expanded at the speed of light; but what did the individual actually achieve, with what precise contribution to that success? The important thing is to discover the truth rather than accept what appears to be so.

While the academic qualifications of salespeople are usually of less value than 'real-world' experience, it is important to substantiate them and check for relevance. Maybe the candidate is lying and didn't get a first at Oxford. Such failure is less important than the reason for avoiding the truth. Maybe the candidate's arts degree does not imply the degree of numeracy required for your particular product or market-place? Maybe your experience shows that only graduates make it with your company in the long-term; so the usefulness of the applicant's single 'O' level in geography is likely to be limited to journey planning. If you know that academic qualifications are essential for your kind of business, check them out; it shouldn't take long to establish their validity. If the candidate is, or has been, involved in further education such as night-school, it tells you something about the person's industry and commitment as well as training and qualifications.

Of course, work experience is of far greater relevance than academic study; but the interviewer should not limit consideration to experience which is directly related to the requirements of the job in question. Maybe the applicant has a successful track record of selling in the electronics industry, while your business is selling high technology medical equipment. The important consideration is whether the candidate has the confidence and mental faculty for selling in a technical environment, perhaps involving complex technical specifications. You have to remember that fully sales-trained candidates with successful track-records are always hard to come by and it takes a year or two to produce a fully trained salesperson. Product-training, on the other hand, no matter how complex the business, seldom takes more than a few months to give an understanding of the basic essentials.

While we are on this topic, I would like to air a particular opinion of mine, that I hasten to add is not merely a subjective whim, but rather an observation gained from many years in sales management and particularly recruitment.

There is a fairly common belief among sales managers in technical selling that articulate technicians make good salespeople. Sadly, this is far from the truth. I can understand the self-comforting belief, particularly if the sales manager comes from a technical background, and especially in an industry where good salespeople are hard to find, but it can lead to some fairly miserable disasters. One of the biggest mistakes we make in life is working on the assumption that the world is populated by clones of ourselves; same intelligence, integrity, industry, commitment, etc. etc., as ourselves. 'If I can make it so can they!' Not necessarily so; in fact, most probably not. You almost certainly got to your position in the company because you are special, above average in the qualities that matter. You made it because of essential human qualities like hard work and common sense, not because you were a qualified and experienced technician. It not only takes longer to become fully fluent in selling than in any product, to build up the essential instincts of selling psychology, organization and self-discipline; but it also calls for particular personal characteristics without which sales success will always be out of reach. It is most important to realize that the learning curve of effective selling is not only long but for many it is a journey that cannot be completed. Common sense dictates that the lesser risk is to put experienced sales recruits through the shorter and more predictable route of product training.

If you insist that your product, applications and industry are too complex for any outsider to grasp within an acceptable time-frame, then do at least take the precaution of having such candidates checked for vocational suitability (see Chapter 7). Remember, it's not academic skills that get a salesperson out of bed at 6 a.m. on a wet December morning to drive up to Barrow-in-Furness, it's the discipline of knowing it's the right thing to be done at the right time in order to ensure ultimate sales success.

So much for relevant experience. The candidate may have sold your kind of product before, experienced your kinds of applications, worked in your industry; but what matters is the candidate's actual accomplishments rather than past responsibilities and future potential. Having sold successfully for past employers, the chances are he or she can do it again for you. If success has constantly proved elusive for reasons that are apparently beyond his or her control, the chances are it will continue to do so.

### 3. Interests

What kind of interests does the candidate have? Are they active, passive, practical, creative—any at all? Consider the nature of those activities the candidate voluntarily pursues in leisure time, for they are likely to give you an insight to the real character within. A heavy commitment to social work may imply a caring and communicative person. On the other hand it might mean that the applicant's outside interests do not allow enough time and attention for a full-time selling job. You need to find out. All the same, it is not always easy to decide how relevant such interests are in the context of a particular job situation. Some people go for high risk sports like caving and hang-gliding, others prefer to pursue interests that allow them to remain apart from the herd, even in isolation. Yet, it does have some bearing on the character of the individual and how he or she is likely to fit within your sales team and the company environment. You need to consider such factors rather than skimming over them with no more than academic interest. Open-ended questions (the ones that start with how, which, why, what, where and when?) are the order of the day.

### 4. Intelligence

In most interview situations, intelligence is quantified to no greater depth than a general impression.

Certainly, some aspects of intelligence can be perceived by studying the performance of the interviewee, such as ease in following the conversation; having a good sense of humour; a quick mind; a sharp wit; common sense. All of these are good indicators of a person's intelligence. Take a closer look at the candidate's academic achievements and outside interests. Did he or she take 'O' and 'A' level examinations at an early age and at what pass level? Brighter kids tend to take their examinations earlier than the others. What subjects were taken? Were they intellectually demanding like sciences and languages or more physically inclined like woodwork, physical education, etc.?

What about sports and hobbies? Do they call for special skills or demand a creative flair? Is this person a doer or a watcher? Any part-time job? Any involvment in communal activity such as social work or participation in any kind of club or society? In what kind of role? Active or passive? Does it call for initiative or does it merely involve following instructions? If people do work for nothing they usually do so because they like it, and they like it because it satisfies their natural tendencies. Such information is usually an insight to the real person that even the candidate does not appreciate.

### 5. Aptitude

This topic has been covered to some degree elsewhere in this book. However, it is essential that the interviewer is aware of those aptitudes that are necessary if salespeople are to succeed. Do they need to be quick with figures, creative, technically perceptive, and so on? What vocational skills are necessary? It is the interviewer's job to ask the right kind of questions and explore the right avenues in order to establish the likely presence or absence of such talents. This can only be done if the vocational requirements are established before interviews take place, and candidate's experience and qualifications are investigated accordingly.

### 6. Disposition

I have already discussed some of the means of identifying the real person behind the interviewee's facade. However, it is just as important to have a clear picture of the kind of person who will fit into your existing team and flourish under your particular style of management. The process of candidate evaluation is not limited to finding out what they are like; just as important is deciding whether or not they are right for your company.

What kind of behaviour can you expect from this applicant? Does his or her record and manner during the interview suggest loyalty, self-motivation, discipline, and conscientiousness? Do you get an impression of ambition, industriousness, tolerance, caring? Don't expect any clear-cut answers. No matter how many times you interview a candidate, you will get no more than an impression; a reasonable idea of what they are really like. It will take at least three to six months of working 'shoulder-to-shoulder' before you really get to know who you took on board. To a great extent you have to rely on your instincts, and sometimes they let you down.

### 7. Health

The candidate's state of health is most important because it has an obvious bearing on ability to pursue the job. No matter how talented a person may be, their accomplishments will be very limited without the energy or health to do a full day's work every working day of the year.

You need to be sure that the candidate is fit. (Not to mention your existing team members!) This can be perceived, to a great extent, from a person's manner, appearance and outside interests. However, nothing beats sending the selected applicants for a medical check, for looks can be deceptive. Fat people aren't necessarily lazy; it's just a nasty rumour put about by thin people who haven't any energy!

## 8. Personal circumstances

One of the most prevalent reasons for under-performance by salespeople, and indeed all working people, is the adverse influence of their social and domestic circumstances. Very often the most talented people are held back because of their home environment.

What about the candidate's family situation? Does it place any restriction upon his or her ability to pursue the job with all the flexibility that selling demands? Are there specific times that he or she must be home? What about the demands of taking children to and from school? One needs, to understand the implications of such a situation completely.

What about the domestic environment? It is balanced and supportive or is it fraught with emotional upset that is likely to impair the candidate's performance?

Does he or she live alone, have children, have the confidence and comfort of sharing hopes, love and anxieties with someone who cares? It is difficult, virtually impossible, to suffer the loneliness of the long-distance salesperson without a firm foundation of domestic security.

What about travelling? The previous sales territory may never have involved more than a couple of hours' travel from home; but the one you are discussing now may involve national responsibility and the necessity to stay away from home, perhaps several nights a week. What about the family's ability to tolerate that? What about the applicant's own ability to cope with it? Have all the implications of the job really been considered? You have to be certain that they have.

The new territory may be even more inconvenient because it means relocating to another part of the country, uprooting home and family. A move south could mean buying a house costing twice as much as his or her present home. Perhaps the children are deeply involved in GCSE examinations and the disruption will be too much for them. The horrors of packing all their belongings into a van and moving to some place where they have no friends or social contact may be too much to contemplate. Perhaps the aspiring employee hasn't really thought it through. Maybe—and don't laugh, because it happens all the time!—the family hasn't been informed about this impending change of employment. You would be surprised how many salespeople accept jobs, then change their mind at the last minute for this very reason, the interviewer must be sure that the applicant understands all the implications of moving home rather than risk all the aggravation and demotivational problems of having them realize it after commencing employment.

Another thing to watch out for is outside interests, both social and business. I have already mentioned their bearing on the nature of the individual, but it is also important to discover if the pursuit of these interests has even the slightest clash with those of the job and the company. A healthy cynicism for the kind of assurances you receive will not be misplaced, particularly when it comes to outside business interests. The freedom of action enjoyed by salespeople makes it easier for them than for most other employees to do 'a bit on the side' in the company's time and even using its resources. The company car and telephone are particularly vulnerable to misuse by those whose activities are not entirely devoted to the company's best interests.

My advice is to avoid such people, but if you are prepared to tolerate this kind of activity, be sure you do so with a very sharp eye and a very short rein.

### 9. Conclusions

Clearly, the basic considerations of candidate evaluation will vary from job to job. It is up to interviewers to decide in advance which are the most important. This means they must be well prepared for every interview, know precisely what they have to discover and fully appreciate that no two candidates are ever the same.

One final point for sales managers who find it difficult to make time for recruitment interviews. There's always plenty of time before 9 a.m. and after 5.30 p.m. Many hard-working salespeople actually prefer it. Indeed, their willingness to attend an out-of-hours interview can be a good measure of their attitude and commitment.

# 6.

# Types of salespeople

'O wad some Pow'r the giftie gie us
To see oursels as others see us!'

*Robert Burns 1759–96*

## 'Skinners and hunters'

Dividing people into broad categories is always a risky business for it serves to overlook the special characteristics of the individual and in doing so, often creates a situation where everyone conforms to the rule as well as being an exception to it. This is particularly true of salespeople who, coming as they do in endless variety, tend to be rather difficult to segregate into a limited range of types.

Despite this, I often find myself dividing salespeople into those about whom I feel either positive or negative, in order to come down to a kind of vocational distillation that contains those most likely to succeed: experienced/inexperienced; trained/untrained; product knowledge/no product knowledge; applications knowledge/no applications knowledge; career progressing/career static; over quota/under quota; mobile/immobile; creative/non-creative; industrious/lazy; communicative/non-communicative; outgoing/introspective, and so on. However, one division that I am always hesitant about is reactive/proactive, for it is easy to assume that the only salespeople able to make a real contribution to company success are the assertive ones.

Consequently, for the benefit of my own objectivity I have always divided salespeople into 'Skinners' and 'Hunters'. I do this to improve my perception of the valid contribution that can be made by those whose very nature makes new-account selling an unavoidable drudge rather than the stimulating challenge it represents to the truly first-class salesperson.

'Hunters' go into the world to seek their 'prey', not occasionally and primarily for creating the right personal image, but instinctively and continually. They travel far and wide, not just around the block; pursuing only relevant objectives, never lost causes; dispatching each willing victim swiftly and caringly; bringing home new sustenance for the family.

'Skinners' wait for the hunter's return. They usually have a good relationship for they have no apparent conflict of interests, neither of them has serious aspirations towards the role of the other.

The 'spoils of the chase' are handed over, and the 'skinners', often with greater dexterity than the 'hunters', not only prepare it for use but may enhance it beyond its basic potential. They may even admire the accomplishments of the 'hunter', but don't have any real inclination to go out and lend a hand!

Unfortunately, many 'skinners', despite the passive nature of their day-to-day activity, secretly believe themselves to be 'hunters'. They see the 'skinner' role as being entirely optional, a transient situation, a force of circumstance that can be taken or left alone. They believe they are able to transcend into the 'hunter/killer' role whenever events demand it, but when they appear to do this, their conversion is always transient. Even their view of hunting is different from that of the 'hunter', for they see it as an unfortunate necessity. 'Skinners' could never hunt for sport.

I believe there is a need in every sales force for both 'skinners' and 'hunters'. The role and personality of the account manager is by necessity very different to that of the new account salesperson.

The trick is to ensure that the 'skinners' are employed in skinning and the 'hunters' are hunting, for otherwise only failure can ensue. There is no point in having a hut full of 'skinners' if there is nobody out there hunting! There is no point in looking for the 'skinner/hunter' hybrid either; there are too few of them around to make the search worth while. Salespeople are usually one or the other, with the exception that 'hunters' can usually skin moderately well, whereas all that 'skinners' are likely to come home with is the bow and arrows they took with them; or at best a bluebird that just happened to fall out of a tree.

It really is a useful and interesting exercise to analyse one's sales team on this basis, but the truth cannot be discovered by direct questioning. Few will admit to being a 'skinner'. The truth can only be found via the prospect list, the number of face-to-face new-account visits, the proportion of new business billing and the opinion of the salesperson's previous employer. In fact, if you are not sure which are the 'hunters', they probably aren't.

## Backing losers

Losers, in the context of selling, are those people who have the perpetual knack of snatching defeat from the jaws of victory. They are those salespeople who inevitably fail you, the sales team and themselves, for a variety of reasons. They can come in many forms; inept, layabouts, freeloaders, cheats, liars, rogues, even outright criminals. However, these labels are invariably applied after the event with the help of that exact science, hindsight. Very often, they are substitutes for earlier and more promising descriptions such as 'Obvious potential in need of a second chance'/'Only needs the right product or company'/'Some problems, but I can sort them out'/'High-flyer or super-hero in need of a change!'

Everybody expects that an experienced professional recruitment consultant should be better than the typical manager at evaluating people. After all, it's a full time occupation for the consultant, whereas most managers spend only a small proportion of their time interviewing potential employees. However, the difference in ability to select the right person for the right job is only marginal. In reality, the recruitment consultant is just as likely to get it wrong as the sales manager. The reason why is very simple. There are no infallible techniques for identifying and qualifying basic human characteristics like industry, integrity and common sense. Psychometric evaluation can be very helpful, but provides no guarantees. Consequently, it is a mistake to rely absolutely on the judgement of external recruitment consultants. The only way one can establish the true nature of such qualities is by extended personal exposure. It is therefore a source of continuing astonishment to me that very few companies go to the trouble of thoroughly reference-checking potential employees. When taxed with such dereliction of duty, the most common excuse is that 'The only pertinent reference is the applicant's current boss, and one cannot reasonably approach that person while the applicant is still in his or her employment!' Fine, but, why not make the job offer subject to satisfactory references from a present employer once the job has been taken up? Few take the trouble to take up this simple but effective assurance. Clearly, any candidate objecting to such an arrangement is like to be hiding something, and is best avoided.

Most sales teams have a loser hiding somewhere in the ranks. The problem is how to identify them.

I believe there are two kinds of loser: honest and dishonest. While both show many warning signals in common, those of the latter are usually the more difficult to identify. The symptoms of the honest incompetent are usually overt as opposed to the subvert characteristics of the congenital malingerer, as he consciously attempts to 'take you for a ride'.

It would take forever to go into the details of all the possible permutations of characteristics, situations, attitudes, etc. that can prevail with the loser syndrome, but here are a few to watch out for:

*Suspicious absence*     On occasions, employees simply fail to show up for work. No forewarning or even any contact at all; they simply disappear. If they do call the office to explain the reason is usually something to do with ill-health. Typically, when they eventually report for duty, their excuse for being absent is either very elaborate or extremely lame. In reality, they may be sleeping off a hangover, feel they can't cope with the job, or simply couldn't face the world today.

*Consistent exceptions*     For some reason one is always having to make exceptions for such people. Agreeing late delivery of reports, non-standard car arrangements, advances against salary and so on. That is usually because they are so disorganized or busy creating a subterfuge for their activity—or lack of it—that they find themselves unable to fit into the normal scheme of things.

*Continual bad luck*     Somehow, success manages constantly to escape the loser. The competition offers dramatic discounts, special features, faster delivery and the like. And then there's that amorphous and irresistible excuse, politics, always politics. They never see themselves as failures. They firmly believe their lack of success is entirely due to the fates giving them a bad time.

*Unconvincing expenses*    Dishonest losers always make expense claims that fall into a different pattern from that of the rest of the sales team. Their cars often use more petrol than those of their colleagues, they always get involved in more of those expenses for which one does not normally get a receipt, they lose receipts, they have lots of receipts from the same garage in the same (and often familiar!) writing, their expenses never tie up with the pattern of sales activity and so on.

*Bad communicators*    Good communications is bad news for people with something to hide. Losers usually produce sketchy and inconsistent call-reports, if they produce them at all. They're the kind of people the sales manager is constantly chasing for call-reports, which they keep promising to produce in the hope that they will eventually be unnecessary or forgotten.

*Jam tomorrow*    Losers are constantly on the verge of some big deal which at a single stroke will recover their shortfall on sales target and recover their self esteem. By the time that particular 'bluebird' has gradually diminished to the lost cause it always was, another equally impressive saviour has arrived upon the scene.

*Excuses, excuses*    Dishonest losers usually have a vivid imagination: they need it in order to prolong survival. They are never lost for elaborate excuses whatever the situation. Lies come easy to them, very often to the pathological degree that they start to believe in their own deceptions. I once had the very bad experience of employing such a person. He became so enmeshed in his own lies that he actually got to the point of chasing overdue accounts from clients with whom neither he nor the company had ever done business.

*Dust raisers*    It is necessary to create an impression of industry and activity if you are to survive as a dedicated loser. So, life is always hectic, rushing around 'seeing people' (usually straight from home or on the way back), making lots of phone calls, writing lots of letters, having lots of 'working lunches' and things like that. Sadly, all this work seldom, if ever, generates any business.

*Personal problems*    We all have personal problems from time to time, but losers have more than their share. It's not their fault of course; it's their husband/wife, or the kids, who are dragging them down. So, they really have to spend lots of time sorting it out, taking the kids to school, and things like that.

The list of possible symptoms is endless; though it has to be said that most of them are not unique to malingerers and scroungers. What is special about losers is that they always have at least one of them running at any given time.

It is easy to view this kind of situation at a distance and make the obvious comment that such people should be dismissed right away; but in the subjective environment of working shoulder to shoulder with losers, it is not quite so simple and clear cut. However, if one is constantly on the look out for the classic symptoms, then objectivity is more likely to prevail.

In my experience one's 'gut feeling' can always be trusted. If you suspect that one of your subordinates is cheating, it's almost certain that you are right. Invariably, you discover that what you suspect is but the tip of an iceberg or dishonesty in one manifestation or another. So, act early rather than late, for delay may allow the problems to drift beyond the company to your clients, putting your hard-earned professional credibility at risk. Don't alloy your judgement to be overruled by tolerance, understanding and altruism; for that consideration is the lifeblood of the loser. If you suspect you are being deceived, don't wait in the hope that the problem will go away. Do some spot checking; ask the employee straight, it's the only way. If such confrontation leads to confessions of misdemeanour, don't allow a second chance. I've made that mistake and it hurts! Leopards can't change their spots, whatever guarantees they may make to the contrary.

Thorough and pertinent reference checking is about as near as you'll get to preventing losers getting on board in the first place, but that is not an infallible process. Don't imagine they'll never get into your sales operation, because they will. In fact, you may have one in your team at this very moment; so be on your guard!

## 'Swinging the lead'

For those who never got around to reading maritime history, it might be useful to explain that in bygone days, when ships attempted to navigate shallow waters, they used a lead weight on the end of a line to test the depth of the water. This was a simple task requiring very little physical effort on the part of the operator, the weight being swung out in front of the ship, and note taken of the appropriate mark when the line was in a vertical position. As the navigation of shallow water was a fairly hazardous business, all able-bodied seamen were obliged to stand at their stations in anticipation of emergency action. Therefore, the job of 'swinging the lead' was usually given to someone who was only fit for light work; which made it a very attractive mode of employment for the scrounger and the work-shy. Consequently, anyone who complained of feeling unwell with no apparent symptoms, was assumed to be contriving to secure the job of checking for depth. Hence, 'swinging the lead'.

Of course, human nature never changes and the proportion of the population who would prefer to 'swing the lead' as opposed to doing a full day's work for a full day's pay, is no less now than it was in the days of sail. Likewise, salespeople (the pun was accidental!) have no less capacity for work-avoidance than those in other occupations.

Within most sales teams there is usually at least one individual who is not 'pulling his weight' (like a team of sailors pulling on a rope, it's easy for the lazy one to pretend they're working just as hard as everyone else) or, to complete this collection of nautical analogies, 'coasting along' if they think they can get away with it. (You know, stay in the calm and shallow waters rather than getting out into the deep and rough stuff where all the real action is.) Such people are not usually identifiable by blatant acts of neglect or laziness, it is more an accumulation of apparently trivial situations that gradually make you realize that everything is not as it should be.

I recall the situation of a salesman who worked for me when I ran the sales operation of a large international computer services bureau. He was very intelligent and articulate, with a lot of selling experience before he joined our company; so much so that he became a kind of unappointed 'guru' to some of the younger and more impressionable members of the selling team. The existence of an unofficial sales counsellor for the junior salesmen did not worry me at all; indeed, senior salespeople should always be encouraged to assist their junior colleagues wherever possible. My real concern was that I didn't feel comfortable about the situation for reasons I couldn't explain. Consequently, I decided to review his past activities and keep a close eye on him. My initial findings appeared to be trivial. His company car consistently did significantly less mileage per gallon than everyone else with identical models. He was the one who always managed to lose his expense receipts. On some occasions, when he couldn't be found and I tried to make urgent contact with him via his wife, he would answer the phone himself, explaining that he had 'just happened to pop into the house' at the time I called. His prospect list was very slow in developing, and his new business revenue was mostly made up of a couple of 'bluebirds' that had fallen into his lap. After some poking around I got a much clearer picture of his approach to the job. Every morning he took his kids to school and most days he collected them again. Friday afternoon working was unknown to him. Yet, his call-reports described a range and quantity of client visits that could only have been achieved by someone working a consistent ten-hour day. Of course, I sacked him, there was no point in threats or edicts. The man had declared his real character by his very actions, and in my experience people don't change.

After the event I wondered how I could have been such a fool as to allow my dauntless tolerance to be exploited in such a way, and vowed to learn from the experience, but that is easier said than done. Most of us tend to think the best of other people until they let us down. This is both a strength and a weakness that the dishonest and inadequate instinctively exploit.

## A bit on the side

To succeed as a sales manager, you must motivate your sales people by displaying a variety of constructive attitudes and qualities that will inspire your team to act likewise. Integrity, enthusiasm, objectivity and industry are qualities that quickly spring to mind; but the one that probably counts for most is commitment.

The salesperson who is not one hundred per cent committed to product, company, team and sales manager, can develop into a difficult problem. Clients and colleagues can quickly discern when someone's heart is not in their job; and this can be a very demotivating influence. Why should one buy from a salesperson whose commitment to the job is questionable? If your colleagues are not giving the job everything they've got, there is always a temptation to do likewise. This can soon lead to all kinds or problems if the situation is allowed to continue.

Of course it is difficult to gain a quick perception of why an individual is giving less than his or her best. Domestic problems? Selling difficulties? Health problems? Looking for alternative employment? The list is endless; but the thing that seldom occurs to the sales manager is the possibility that one of the sales team might have another job at the same time. Hard to believe perhaps; but probably more common than one might imagine.

Salespeople, being the entrepreneurial breed they are, represent the occupational group most likely to get involved in a 'bit (or even a lot!) on the side'. Consider the following possibilities:

## 'Moonlighting'

Most salespeople have access to additional employment outside the normal working hours of their employer, should the need or inclination arise. The variety of potential jobs is enormous, as a part-time employee or a freelancer. Working in the bar of the local pub, selling services and products such as insurance, unit trusts, double glazing, encyclopaedias and domestic products, part-time teaching, mini-cab driving, etc. etc.

## 'Piggy-back' commission

Depending on the type of product, industry and market-place there is considerable scope for salespeople to sell additional goods outside their employer's product arena. If, for instance, one is selling a range of products to computer users that is limited to magnetic media, there is a lot of opportunity for selling items such as computer-room furnishings, listing-paper, printer-ribbons, tape-cleaners, etc. on a commission-only basis. Given the opportunity, some salespeople may find the temptation too great, resulting in an ethical compromise.

## 'The spouse's own business'

Many salespeople have enterprising spouses who quite independently run their own business and do so on the understanding that their partner has no involvement, simply because they prefer it that way. There's no harm in that! However, there are others who merely act as a front for the entrepreneurial activities of their partners, or who entirely rely upon them for various aspects of their business operation. This could involve the salesperson in many unofficial tasks including selling, buying, collecting stock, keeping the accounts and so on, all time and energy-consuming activities that are likely to be to the detriment of an employer.

Such enterprise inevitably involves customers and suppliers whose business hours correspond with those of the salesperson's employer. Consequently, one can never be sure that each urgent sales visit and every extended long-distance telephone call is necessarily in pursuit of the company's best interest—at least, not yours!

## *Pre-self-employment*

Ask salespeople about their ambitions and the chances are they will say they want to be a sales manager or set up their own business. Unfortunately many salespeople who decide to go it alone contrive to bring about a considerable overlap with their present employment. The temptation to keep working a couple of days a week for one's present employer and hang on to the basic salary and company car is quite considerable. It doesn't take much effort and imagination to falsify call-reports, expenses, prospect-lists, etc. to give the impression of doing a fair day's work. With a little ingenuity, it's possible to string an employer along for many months. Sales managers who are out of touch with the field are very susceptible to this kind of deception.

The effect of such activities are obvious. Achieving sales target is a difficult enough task at the best of times, but if salespeople are diverting their energies elsewhere, they have little chance of success. More importantly, if they are prepared to involve themselves in such deception, they are clearly not the kind of people you want in your team.

This kind of activity must be nipped in the bud. Any form of external business for reward, be it for another company or self-employment, should be strictly forbidden and expressly stated in each salesperson's service contract from the very beginning. Any employee who breaks this ruling should be instantly dismissed, even if only to focus the thinking of others who might be considering similar activities. It must be absolutely clear to all employees that the company is only interested in employing people who are totally committed to the achievement of its objectives. If they cannot give such an undertaking, the only available course is to invite them to find a company who doesn't require a hundred per cent commitment from its employees. The chances are they will be looking for a long time.

Let me tell you some true stories.

A few years ago I was carrying out a recruitment assignment for a major computer manufacturer. During the process of interviewing, I happened upon an applicant whose experience and accomplishments were so impressive that I could not understand why he had applied for the job concerned. In fact, he appeared to be so good that I became suspicious.

He was running his own business at the time I interviewed him, so I decided to check him out with his previous employer, a mini-computer manufacturer, where I knew the personnel manager quite well. 'Steer clear of that one!' was the reply, 'We are currently taking legal action against him for fraudulent conversion. Apart from other things, he was running his own full-time business at the same time as he was supposed to be working for us, simply living off the guaranteed income he had negotiated from us and using the company car to pursue his own business!' I was shocked, but not as surprised as I might have been. I was about to ring off when he continued, 'And that's not all. At the same time as he was working for us he was also posing as a salesman for another computer manufacturer. They're taking legal action too!' That's right, that job also included a guaranteed basic income and a company car. Well, his wife had to drive something!

Then there's the story I got from a friend and well-respected competitor of mine in the sales recruitment business. Apparently he had a strange telephone call from a client of his, enquiring about a particular man, who, for the sake of discretion, I will call Bill Smith. (Sorry, Bill!)

My friend is in the business of recruiting salespeople related to high technology products. One day, he received a telephone call from one of his clients.

'You know Bill Smith don't you?'

My friend was immediately on his guard, for he quickly identified Smith as one of the biggest rogues in the business and not to be touched at any price, even with a specially extended barge-pole.

'Yes?' he replied hesitantly.

There was an awkward silence, which the caller eventually but very tentatively, broke.

'Bit of a rogue isn't he?'

My friend admitted that it seemed to be common opinion in the business.

'Actually I've known about this character for a few years myself.'

His client began to gain in confidence as we went on with his story.

'I'm told he's ripped off company after company; that he's utterly dishonest, totally unreliable and completely incompetent.'

'Why are you telling me all this?' asked my friend, by this time becoming increasingly suspicious.

'You know I've got this glass-sided office?' explained the caller. 'Well, I'm looking out across the department as I'm speaking to you and I've just realized who's sitting at one of the sales desks. I'm afraid Bill Smith now works for us!'

In complete contrast, my final story is about a Managing Director who was very successfully appointed to take over an ailing high technology company. In three years he took the company from revenues of less than £2 million to almost £20 million. But that is what everyone had hoped for, indeed some expected, from a man of such high qualifications, previous experience and achievement.

Unfortunately, on the way home from an executive management meeting where the booze had flowed a bit too liberally, he was arrested for drunken driving. As a result, his real background somehow emerged. It transpired that his experience and qualifications were a fabrication from beginning to end. More particularly, he had no previous senior management experience at all. In fact, immediately prior to joining this company, he had been a milkman! (Don't ask me what they did or didn't do about reference checking.) A lot of heavy discussion and embarrassment ensued within the main board, but the 'blind-eye' lobby won the day. For all I know he's still there today. Perhaps there's a moral in that story?

# 7.

# *Vocational suitability*

---

'Walk worthy of the vocation wherewith ye are called'

*Holy Bible (Ephesians)*

### Getting on the right track

One of the best decisions I ever made was to call upon the professional advice of a vocational analyst for career guidance. This involved the use of well-proven methods of personality assessment, which are able to address most aspects of human character, thus enabling a well-informed judgement to be made in the context of suitability for a particular job. Armed with this objective analysis, I was able to step out of the lemming run and ask myself whether I was really making the best of my life in general and my career in particular.

Up until this point I had survived the journey from sales trainee to salesman, to regional sales manager, to national sales manager, to sales and marketing director, and then European general manager. To the world at large I appeared to be a very successful man. The only problem was that life was fast becoming all work and no play, with one plastic hotel, one stale airport waiting-lounge, one twelve-hour working day becoming much the same as another. I knew I was doing a good job, but it was beginning to cost me a lot socially, domestically, physically and mentally, even though I believed I was enjoying the demands and stimulation of my occupation. The insidious toll of stress was becoming apparent, certainly to me and most probably to everyone around me.

Then, one day, after a bitter confrontation with my peers, it occurred to me that perhaps I could be doing something better with my talents. The problem was, I didn't really know what they were. It also struck me that any appraisal of my capabilities and vocational potential by colleagues and friends would be just as subjective, and therefore as prone to error, as my own.

It was at this point that I decided to seek the guidance of a professional vocational guidance consultant.

Having completed the appropriate psychometric questionnaires (one would expect to use a microcomputer nowadays!) and a subsequent interview, the consultant proceeded to tell me about my strengths and weaknesses. I prepared myself for some startling revelations, but there were none. Everything he said was very familiar. The consultant's perceptions gave the impression that he had been speaking to my mother. Nothing was a surprise, other than the fact that he should know so much about me in so short a time. In effect, he held a mirror to my face and said 'This is you!', and it was. There before my very eyes were the personal truths I had chosen to ignore, or allowed circumstances to divert from my attention.

As is often the case with psychometric analysis, I was not asked about my current occupation. So, when some of my weaknesses aparently coincided with the demands of my current job, I questioned the outcome, protesting that in terms of my achievements and the reaction of my peers, I was successful.

The consultant was not at all surprised by my reaction. He told me that my statement did not in any way contradict his findings. He explained that, in general terms, any intelligent, hard-working person could be successful in virtually any job. However, the vocationally unsuitable person, i.e. the one without the natural aptitude, has to put in considerably more effort for the same result as the one who is right for the job. As good a recipe as any for a premature heart attack!

I don't believe in paying for sensible professional advice and then ignoring it. So, I backed out of the career cul-de-sac that ambition had diverted me into and got back onto what I perceived to be the main highway of my vocational destiny. I returned to those things I had left behind because I thought them insufficiently demanding for my talents and ambition. In reality they only seemed easy because I was good at them; they suited my natural talents. It was obvious I was back on the right track because the subsequent journey was like freewheeling, as opposed to grinding away in first gear from dawn till dusk in order to achieve a performance level that was acceptable to my self-inflicted standards.

Perhaps you have seen other people in this kind of situation? In to work early, working through lunch-break, staying late at the office; yet without ever really achieving outstanding performance. Maybe you are in the same situation yourself? Are you sure you're in the right slot? Life is too short to spend it thrashing around in order to keep your head above water in the wrong occupation; especially when you can be skimming along in the right one. For me it was as if I had been mentally reborn. I felt like an evangelist spreading the word of my vocational release to others who seemed trapped in the wrong job. I guess that's what got me into the recruitment and training business, and eventually into psychometric analysis.

There are so many people in selling who really shouldn't be in the job at all. More often than not they survive by virtue of being in a seller's market, or because of a reputation stemming from some bygone windfall. People are not always what they seem. Judging them purely by their results and subjective observation is a very inefficient and misleading process. The failure of individual salespeople is often as much the fault of inept management and inadequate products, as it is an absence of the appropriate human characteristics. The reasons for failure can be extremely complicated. It is therefore very surprising that most personnel selection, particularly related to salespeople, is limited to the subjectivity of the face-to-face interview.

A study carried out by a well-known British psychometrician into a wide range of methods of personnel evaluation, from palmistry to selection panels, declared the typical recruitment interview to be some 19 per cent reliable, i.e. some 81 per cent unreliable. While the quality and efficiency of interviews can vary considerably, the statistics give some idea of how much we can rely upon the interview within the process of putting the right person into the right job.

Because of this inefficient selection process the 'articulate layabout' and the 'well-informed failure' are able to survive on a sales career of 'guarantee-hopping' and other means of keeping one step ahead of failure. On the other hand, there must be a multitude of salespeople working very hard and achieving moderate success who could be much happier and successful in some other occupation—if only they knew what it was!

## Identifying individual strengths and weaknesses

The possible variations of human characteristics are endless. Some may be regarded as strengths, others as weaknesses; depending on individual performance, self-perception and the opinion of the beholder.

Whatever impression each of us gives to the world, we are likely to see ourselves differently, if only because we spend more time contemplating the subject than anyone else. But that does not necessarily imply our interpretation is the most accurate one. Very often the onlooker sees more of the game than the player, and in the context of self-evaluation, subjectivity can be a very strong diversion from reality. Yet, most people have what they believe to be a reasonable understanding of who they are and where they are going. They observe their talents and their shortcomings, and instinctively emphasize the first and conceal the second. Sadly, accurate self-analysis with all its subjective limitations, is the most difficult task in the world. Consequently, many of us spend our lives without any real understanding of our talents and vocational suitability. We become a complex tangle of strengths, weaknesses, ambitions and mistakes, confused by the capriciousness of circumstances. Most of us have yet to discover who we really are.

It is within this kind of scenario that the sales manager goes about the task of selecting the right people for the sales team; not totally self-aware, and without the benefit of the kind of deep understanding of another human being that only comes from many months, or even years, of face-to-face exposure. It is a very imprecise business, fraught with risk, where more than fifty per cent success is an outstanding achievement. It is a highly subjective process, where clones of oneself can become, unconsciously, the ideal candidate profile.

Even people such as social workers and the clergy, who devote their lives to understanding other people, make mistakes all the time. In fact, they will be the first to tell you how difficult it is to assess the nature of the individual. Therefore, the chances of the typical sales manager getting it right all the time, when selection and recruitment normally represent a very small proportion of his or her overall activity, are so remote as to be non-existent.

If only there were some way of obtaining complete insight to the real person behind the facade that is inevitably presented in the interview situation, what a tremendous asset that would be. When one considers the cost of recruiting the wrong salespeople, in terms of lost revenues and unhappy clients, it would be worth a lot of money.

Well, there is no absolutely certain methodology that can provide totally accurate facts on human characteristics; but over the years psychometricians have been able to develop systems which can give a meaningful though transient perception of individual personality; it is called psychometric analysis.

## Psychometric analysis

Personality assessment by the use of psychometric analysis techniques is likely to generate some apprehension, even suspicion and cynicism from sales managers, as well as from those who are to be assessed. Although such techniques have been well proven over many years, their use in personnel selection and development is, at the time of writing, only just becoming a relatively common part of the evaluation process within the more progressive companies. This is perhaps due to a natural distrust of things that are new or not understood.

The function of personality assessment systems is to create a more comprehensive and objective picture of the individual than might otherwise be possible, particularly if the period of evaluation is unavoidably brief. Many of the methods have been designed to enable specific personality factors such as personal organization, persistence, authority-dependence, ambition, assertiveness, social adeptness, and so on, to be isolated and assessed. These usually take the form of multiple-choice questions from which the candidate selects his preferences.

It is important to understand that there are no 'right' or 'wrong' solutions. The correct answer is the one the participant believes to be true.

I hope you will observe that I have studiously avoided the word 'test' as in 'psychometric test'. The word 'test' tends to imply precise measurement, like getting twelve out of twenty in the end-of-term maths examinations when the pass mark is fifteen. You failed! *No one ever passes or fails personality assessment!* The objective is to discover what kind of person you are. It may prove to be the case that your characteristics are wrong for a particular post. That means you failed to qualify for the job, you did not fail a psychometric 'test'. You also failed to secure a job that was not suited to your nature, and that can only be good news.

The main objective of psychometric analysis, as far as the potential employer is concerned, is to gain a deeper knowledge of the candidate. However, it also makes it possible to view such qualities in the context of the circumstances surrounding the job concerned. It is therefore essential that the psychometric analyst has a detailed awareness of the role to be performed and all other factors that have a significant influence upon it. Once they are clearly established the analyst is able to select the appropriate psychometric method for providing an insight to the critical personality features and other factors that enable the right match to be made.

Most psychometric analysis systems in use today are well proven. But if the results they give are not properly interpreted and understood they are of little value—indeed, they can be extremely dangerous. This is not a technique to be toyed with by laymen, and sales managers should not be misled into thinking that psychometric analysis is something they can do for themselves, even assuming they have the time. It is a process that demands considerable training and experience before it can be carried out safely and effectively. That does not necessarily imply that only a trained psychologist can understand or provide the service, but it does mean that the capabilities and limitations must be fully appreciated and the skills and experience of interpretation well practised.

The best source for such a service within the more substantial organizations usually resides within the personnel department. Indeed, some of the large corporations have their own psychologists, even their own psychometricians. Nowadays, a large proportion of personnel professionals have psychology degrees and/or extensive experience of interpreting the results of psychometric analysis systems. But, even if there is no one currently trained in personality assessment, there will almost certainly be someone who is keen to get the appropriate training and provide the service for you.

The most important discipline for the trainee psychometric analyst is the avoidance of literal interpretations. The results provided by any personality assessment systems are unlikely to be accurate in the absolute sense. They merely provide well-informed signposts that guide the interviewer towards the status of a particular human characteristic. Only subsequent dialogue offers the posibility of identifying the real truth.

Much myth and mystique surrounds the business of psychometric analysis; but that is to be expected of a science that has never really escaped from its academic origins. A friend of mine once described psychometricians as the 'Guardians of the Black Art'. I have to say that from the outside looking in, that is an understandable impression.

There is also a danger that personality assessment can be perceived as an exact science; not by design but by default. Hence the 'passing or failing syndrome'. It is very important for everyone who is involved with this process to keep a firm grip on reality. The late Professor Ghiselli of the University of California, Berkeley, a major figure in the origins and development of psychometric analysis, concluded that the modal validity coefficient of occupational tests, thus personality tests, so called, is in the range of 0.28 to 0.30, where perfect prediction is 1.0. That's the kind of process we are dealing with, and that is the context in which it must always be used.

I once attended a convention at which one of our companies was exhibiting its psychometric assessment and testing products. (Yes, both types exist and the distinction is important. Psychometric tests can only measure what is absolutely measurable, and personality does not come into this category.) I was approached by a senior executive from a large public organization who wanted to know about our personality assessment products. I asked him what he knew about psychometric analysis and he told me that it was already in use in different sectors of their organization. How did he feel about them? He was a bit hesitant to tell me at first, but it soon became apparent that he was extremely unhappy about their use. In fact, he was very scathing, even hostile, about their unfairness and potential for creating insecurity among employees. I asked him if he had been psychometrically assessed, and he had. How did he get on? 'I don't know,' he said, 'they never tell us!'

That kind of situation must be avoided at all costs. It is the very essence of how personality assessment should not be used, because it is, as I have already stated, an inexact and potentially unreliable science, and nothing is more worrying, demotivating and unsettling than simply not knowing.

Personality assessment must only be used as a precursor to face-to-face interview, otherwise it is worthless. Only subsequent dialogue can reveal the true meaning of sometimes uncannily accurate results, that nonetheless need to be interpreted in the context of individual circumstances. Many vendors of psychometric 'tests', as they invariably call them, attempt to prove the reliability and therefore the value of their products by providing reams of statistical information, thus propagating the impression that they are marketing an absolute science for accurately identifying hidden truths. Professor Ghiselli's findings provide a more meaningful perspective; as indeed does the more recent research of Dr Mike Smith of the University of Manchester Institute of Science and Technology who was prepared to go as far as 0.35 for the typical reliability coefficient of personality assessment systems.

'Real world' psychologists are likely to take a more pragmatic view. I once had a very interesting conversation with an eminent psychometrician about the various types of statistical validation that are applied to personality assessment— 'test-retest reliability' and all that kind of stuff. He explained their relative importance; but when we got to the matter of overall reliability in terms of accurately assessing an inventory of human characteristics, he said 'Self perception analysis [that's just another name for the same thing] is only as valid as the recipient believes it to be.'

That struck me as a very perceptive and common sense evaluation of what is fast becoming an everyday personnel selection tool. Certainly, the question of predictive reliability is a source of considerable anxiety for those who are on the receiving end of an ever-increasing selection of psychometric offerings.

Of course, there can be a significant disparity between what an interviewee believes and what he or she will admit to; that is why an effective interviewing technique and an emphathic manner are crucial in the successful assessment of personnel.

An interesting aspect of basic human characteristics is that some are permanent and others are transient. For instance, if people are untidy around the office and at home, the chances are that they have always been the same and always will be. Whereas, their ambition will fluctuate according to whatever stage their career has reached, whether or not they have had a recent promotion, whether or not they are currently in employment, and so on. So, the profile given by a personality assessment system at any particular time, may not be a valid statement of the true nature of the individual as he or she might be in other or more normal circumstances.

For instance, a salesperson whose profile indicates very little self-motivation is unlikely to enjoy further consideration for a selling job. Without it, how can anyone succeed in selling? But this is an unstable characteristic that can be radically affected by prevailing circumstances. Transient events can have an adverse effect on personal disposition. Yet, these demotivating circumstances could be alleviated by a variety of factors, from the passing of time to simply getting the job you have on offer. What if he or she

Has recently been bereaved?

Has just recovered from an illness?

Has been out of work for a long period of time?

Has just got divorced?

Was involved in a serious road accident on the way to the interview?

One way or the other, this person's motivation will have been unavoidably affected, and an effective personality assessment system will certainly identify the situation; but more importantly, will also show a change at a later date. So it is essential to find out why, rather than taking the results literally. Otherwise you could be turning down the best salesperson in town who just happens to have had a bit of bad luck.

The use of psychometric assessment is not limited to personnel selection; it can be very valuable in other situations where knowing the nature of the person can make a tremendous difference to making the right decision or providing the right kind of help. For example:

Assessment for promotion or redeployment.

Appraisal of performance and job satisfaction.

Individual counselling.

Assistance in redundancy situations.

Recruiting to a job profile.

## Assessment by personality profiling

Personality profiling is a very useful and relatively simple method of assessing the personal characteristics of potential recruits, in accordance with your own particular needs. It can be used in the context of any job function, as long as you can highlight the key character traits within that particular role, and more importantly, identify the kind of character profile that tends to succeed for you. That can be achieved by assessing those people within your company who are already successful in the role concerned.

The characteristics addressed by the system I am acquainted with, are all related to the individual in the work situation, rather than concentrating on social and domestic factors. You will see that they all have a bearing on how people are likely to perform in their current job.

*Work style*
Intensity of effort
Target orientation
Personal involvement
Organizational skills
Detail orientation
Work rate
Persistence
Rule dependency
Work planning
Need for change

*Leadership qualities*
Leadership style
Delegation
Control of subordinates
Authority dependence

*Decisiveness*
Decision making

*Temperament*
Assertion
Ambition
Impulsiveness
Emotional disposition
Creativity
Dexterity
Energy

*Group interaction*
Dependence on others
Need for acceptance
Need for attention
Social adeptness
Group orientation
Co-operation

*Prospective qualities*
Current leadership ability
Prospective leadership ability
Prospective selling ability

Creativity
Followership
Impulsiveness
Tempo of living
Technical orientation
Self-confidence
Social interaction

However, some of these characteristics are obviously more important than others as far as successful salespeople are concerned. What is more important, these characteristics will vary from one kind of product and market to another; even from company to company. So, if personality profiling is to make a useful contribution to the selection process within your sales organization, you must first ascertain the mix and balance of human characteristics that are common to your accomplished salespeople.

Don't expect all the good people to fit the same profile because they won't. As I have reiterated, personality assessment is not an exact science. Salespeople are individuals like any other people. However, there will be many characteristics that are common and some that are absolutely essential.

So, once all the successful salespeople have been assessed you will be able to create a general sales profile; and I do stress general. You might want to emphasize characteristics for some special sales roles, such as major account management. You may wish to ignore some of the less desirable characteristics of some of your top earners. That's up to you. Eventually, you will have a profile of characteristics within which most of your best people fit.

Having established this generic profile, all you have to do is compare it with the detailed personality assessment of each new applicant and see how that fits. Let me hasten to add that candidates who do not fit within it are not necessarily disqualified; but you do need to know why. Similarly, there is no point in wasting time by discussing those aspects of personality where the applicant's rating is within your requirements. The focus of attention should be on those character-istics that are outside the desired profile. You might call it assessment by exception.

'Lacks self sufficiency.' Why?
'Low work rate.' Why?

These are crucial questions which might never be asked without the help of psychometric analysis. They are also questions which are best addressed obliquely, as the full-frontal approach can easily make the interviewee become self-protective and unlikely to provide the answer you need.

I mentioned a little earlier that I would discuss the relative importance of human characteristics in salespeople.

A validation exercise was carried out on a large number of successful and unsuccessful salespeople from a number of companies selling different kinds of products into a variety of markets. The objective was to validate the accuracy of past personality assessment against subsequent performance. The exercise was performed to everyone's satisfaction, but most importantly, made it possible to identify the most crucial characteristics among those salespeople considered to be successful, and those who were unsuccessful. To everyone's initial surprise the characteristic which provided the biggest differential between the great and the not-so-great, was ambition!

Look through the list of characteristics again and see which one you would have selected to be the key characteristic for salespeople. I must admit, it is not the one I would have chosen at the time; but subsequent consideration enabled me to realize what it really meant. Ambition is but another manifestation of the will to win; wanting to be the best. Anyone who does not have that driving force is unlikely to ever enjoy outstanding sales success.

So much for the nature and scope of psychometric analysis as it relates to the assessment of salespeople; but what is it all worth?

It is simply another weapon in the armoury of personnel selection and development. It is not in itself a panacea to replace other tried and tested methods such as the interview. It merely improves the chances of putting the right person into the right job. From the sales manager's point of view that must lead to higher individual achievement, greater motivation and a happier and more stable sales force. That must inevitably bring greater success for the company, particularly in terms of increased revenues.

## Selecting the wrong people

A regular phenomenon in selling is to witness last year's top salesperson fail in the new position of sales manager; brought down by the realities of the 'Peter Principle'. As Dr Lawrence J. Peter wrote in 1969: 'In a hierachy every employee tends to rise to his level of incompetence.' Psychometric evaluation has been designed to reveal the truths and provide the objectivity to enable people to avoid such a sad, wasteful, avoidable and sometimes humiliating situation.

Occasionally, during a recruitment programme, a candidate will be rejected for no apparent reason. The interviewer just has a hunch, an indefinable worry, and isn't prepared to take the risk. Psychometric testing is often able to highlight the cause of such unease and indicate whether there really should be cause for concern.

Have you ever wondered why apparently outstanding candidates often fail to come up to expectations? Have you also thought that the second- or third-choice candidate might have done better? Objective assessment by psychometric means can help to identify the real 'number one' by breaching the facade that is inevitably presented by the candidate in an interview situation.

It is also important to view the whole sales team in the context of individual talents and personalities. If a manager is aware of the strengths and weaknesses of the team, future planning and development can be carried out in a much more effective manner. For example, a lack of management potential may be identified among the team, and the manager can therefore ensure that the emphasis of future recruitment is upon those with the appropriate talents. At the very least, psychometric analysis of an entire sales team will give the sales manager a better perception of the possibilities and limitations to be coped with, and the best ways to exploit the strengths and offset the weaknesses. More particularly, when it comes to essential management functions like motivation, counselling and appraisal, the whole process becomes much easier when the sales manager has a positive insight to the salesperson's inherent characteristics and current emotional make-up.

## Removing the fear of psychometric analysis

When short-listed for a job, a candidate is usually open-minded about the prospect of personality assessment. That does not mean that all apprehension is dispelled. In some instances the situation will be very much the contrary. But, as such analysis is seen to be part of the recruitment process, the importance placed on it by the prospective employer will be realized and the situation usually approached in a realistic manner. Interest in a vacancy is what makes one apply. If the applicant has the kind of flexibility that is essential in selling, he or she will accept scientific assessment as a necessary qualification, a challenge, and an interesting experience. It is common sense that one should not accept a job to which one is unsuited, or does not represent a positive step towards one's career objectives. In that context, apparent failure is preferable to success. However, one cannot be certain that the candidate is aware of the benefits involved or that he or she has previously experienced psychometric analysis. It is therefore essential that any assessment exercise is prefaced with an informal introduction to the process, stating the objectives and the benefits to both parties, and eradicating any misconceptions of 'right or wrong' and 'pass or fail'.

It is especially important that participants are given this type of explanation when selected people are to be evaluated as opposed to an entire department. Fears of 'bad reports' or using the results as an excuse for dismissal or demotion are unavoidable. Such doubts can never be entirely eliminated. Consequently, the sales manager, or personnel professional must make it clear that every member of the company has the right to be developed to his or her maximum potential, and psychometric analysis is an excellent way of discovering what such potential is likely to be. Surely, such a detailed and objective evaluation must be preferable to the subjective and potentially inconsistent assessment that may otherwise be produced by the sales manager! When presented in the correct manner, most salespeople will rightly interpret the use of psychometric analysis as confirmation of their company's progressive attitude and its willingness to invest in individual career development.

Occasionally, a salesperson may not be sure about the future, having the feeling of not being wholly suited to selling, but unable to think what else to do. In many of these cases psychometric analysis can help to identify career alternatives based on the strengths, weaknesses, and behavioural style of the individual.

However, the total benefits of personality assessment can only be fully achieved by regular use within personnel development as a whole. If a company limits these methods to selection, or individual problem-solving, it may become increasingly difficult to use them as time goes on. Employees can easily gain the impression that psychometric analysis is only for those who are being considered for promotion, or as some means of laying blame when things are going wrong. When there are opportunities for career advancement, those individuals who are not sent for assessment may feel they are no longer being considered for promotion. This can cause resentment and demotivation, and is best avoided. Psychometric analysis is a tool, a means to an end; not an end in itself.

## Faking the results

If you are wondering whether the results produced by personality assessment systems can be faked, the answer has to be yes! Candidates can give the answers they feel the selector wants, rather than the ones that represent their real opinions or preferences. They can condition their responses in order to emphasize those qualities they believe to be important. In a selection situation this is understandable, because applicants are keen to make a favourable impression. However, this will certainly lead to extreme results which will be apparent to the psychometric analyst, particularly when they are discussed in a subsequent interview. For instance, applicants consistently emphasizing their positive managerial qualities are likely to achieve profiles more applicable to Atilla the Hun than to themselves.

Trying to cheat is stupid. After all, the whole point of utilizing character assessment techniques is to help individuals find the right job for their talents. This might not be compatible with their aspirations, but is certainly much more likely to lead to personal fulfilment. That is why it is so important to make the benefits and objectives of psychometric assessment abundantly clear to the participant right from the start.

Nonetheless, candidates are usually unfamiliar with personality assessment systems and the factors they measure, and will therefore be unable to determine the pattern of questioning and the appropriate emphasis of response that is necessary to achieve the desired effect. But neither will they be in a position to know what a 'good' result actually is, and will therefore tend to decide on honesty as the only logical course.

The psychometric analyst should always make it clear that faked responses will certainly do candidates more harm than good, will probably result in destroying any chances they may have of securing the job in question and, even worse, create the risk of obtaining a job where failure is the most likely outcome.

# Appendix

# Sales managers seeking re-employment

'Even God cannot change the past.'

*Agathon c. 401 BC*

### What are the alternatives?

While most sales managers who visit our company come to discuss their sales recruitment needs, some come along to discuss their own career prospects. What are the possible alternatives in terms of discipline, rank, product, market-place, and so on? Are they in the right kind of job? Are their ideas on future possibilities practical? I can't say we always have the right answers, but it is usually helpful to discuss your career problems with someone who has the objectivity of an informed onlooker.

For those who are determined upon the course of staying in sales management but moving to another company, our first task is to ensure that they appreciate that there are always less jobs than sales managers to fill them.

### Trying a change of discipline

Of the many different conversations we have with sales managers on the move, two are particularly recurrent.

'I wish to secure a different kind of job by moving to another company.'

'I would like to set up my own business, but I have yet to think of an original idea or discover an unsatisfied demand to be exploited.'

Some of the most common sales-related examples of people wishing for a change of career direction, are technicians wanting to get into selling, salespeople seeking to advance into sales management status by moving to another company, and sales managers attempting to achieve a higher level of responsibilities by the same means.

When you think about it, these are completely unreasonable expectations. When a company goes outside its own ranks for personnel, it does so to obtain skills that are wholly or partly absent from its own organization. If, for instance, they wish to replace a national sales manager who has left their employment, then they must, by definition, be seeking a replacement with proven national sales management skills and experience, not a manager who has only operated at the regional level or a senior salesman who reckons he or she ought to be in management. It may be true that such people have the talent and potential for enhanced responsibility, but that is not the point. No company can afford the risk of employing a stranger in a key role unless that person already has the skills and experience to succeed in the job, with minimum disruption. If the need is merely one of potential, it is likely that such people are already in the company's employment. The problems are time and risk. The duration and therefore cost, of waiting for someone to gain fluency in a new discipline, as well as getting to know the product, the company, the industry and the market-place is more than most companies can afford. 'Mature trainees' from external sources, in the context of a critical selling environment, seldom offer any attraction for the perceptive employer.

For those who are absolutely determined to advance their status be moving companies, there is likely to be only one possibility, and that is to move 'down market' in terms of company size and stature. Many small companies are prepared to use the influence of job titles to attract people from large organizations. A District Sales Manager from a major manufacturer may be just the man for a distributor who needs a Sales and Marketing Director. Some find the greater freedom of a smaller company very satisfying, others may find the lack of resources limiting and frustrating. It all depends on what you are looking for.

Very often, people wishing to secure a different kind of job or increase their personal status by changing company, do so for reasons of frustration and disillusionment. They can see no way of progressing within their present role or company, and out of sheer desperation decide to move in order to solve the problem. In many cases, this is the only available course; but the mistake many make is expecting a change of employer to bring about an instant freeing of their career potential. What is more, a new job doesn't bring about a change of person-ality. You can't move away from yourself. It is essential to initiate some personal analysis before moving on in the belief that lack of progress was thrust upon you, rather than of your own creation.

Without any doubt, the best chances of advancing personal status and responsibility, or moving to a new kind of job, usually exist within one's present company. If all attempts to progress make it clear there are no real opportunities to pursue one's aspiration, then the only alternative is to move on. However, it only makes sense if such a move is to another company where the new job can be tackled with confidence, by using one's existing skills and experience to achieve early success. It is obviously essential to establish at the interview stage that the job in question provides the opportunity of performing, or advancing, into the kind of occupation you wish to pursue. If subsequent employment does not lead to the satisfaction of your ambitions, you have either chosen the wrong company, or you never really had the talent in the first place!

## Setting up your own business

Setting up your own business is an altogether different affair and many books have been written about the problems and opportunities of establishing your own show. My thoughts are merely aimed at the implications of starting out.

I suspect that most people who say they would like to set up their own business if only they had an original idea, or if they could obtain the necessary finance, do so merely for effect. It is as if they feel obliged to project an entrepreneurial image, or create the impression that they have the drive, talent, enthusiasm and courage to go beyond the less risky position of being an employee—if only the fates were not against them. The fact is, one does not need an original idea to set up a new business, and there is never a shortage of financial backing for a sound business proposition. There are innumerable examples which make it abundantly clear that originality can often be a positive disadvantage. Lord Leverhulme once said words to the effect that 'when establishing a new business, the best course is not to search for a demand that is not being satisfied and satisfy it, but rather to discover where it is being satisfied and satisfy it better.' That is business pragmatism at its most effective. So many companies with novel and revolutionary ideas have failed because they couldn't survive the long and costly 'learning curve' of creating and educating a new market.

The most difficult thing about setting up your own business is 'taking the plunge'. My simple, yet deceptively obvious, advice for those who are determined to go it alone, but are unsure of what they should do, is simply:

'Do what you do best in the industry you know best.'

To do otherwise, to compound the hazards of business survival with the problems of learning a new occupational discipline, or getting to know a new industry or market-place, makes a Kamikaze pilot the very essence of survivalism.

## Returning to the ranks

Sales managers who visit us with the objective of securing a new job are usually surprised to discover that we do not have a mass of job opportunities from which they can select a number of appropriate options. The problem is that most of them have never experienced the process of changing employment at the management level and, having achieved their management status by promotion from territory sales within their present company, expect the availability of jobs to be the same as when they were salespeople. Supply and demand dictate to the contrary. One obvious factor is the reality of the hierarchical company pyramid; the higher it gets the narrower it becomes. There are simply less sales managers around than there are salespeople, thus relatively less job opportunities. A simple analysis of the situation is that up to the level of senior salesperson, there are generally more jobs than competent people to fill them. Above this level, there are always more managers than jobs.

As I have already said, ask most salespeople what their ambitions are and they're likely to say that they want to set up their own business or progress into management. In other words there are always plenty of senior salespeople as well as established managers hustling for any management jobs that are in the offing. From the company point of view it is far more attractive, in a variety of respects, to give a chance to a known employee than bring in a stranger from outside. So the problem for the manager wanting to change companies is that most of the relevant job opportunities never actually get into the public domain.

Look at the situation from a sales director's point of view. If you have to go outside to recruit a sales manager, you are actually making a statement of personal failure to your fellow directors. Your action implies that you are not growing your people or developing their skills. By the same token, you are suggesting to some, or even all of your subordinates, that they are either inadequate or undesirable in the context of promotion; making them insecure and discontented. You will clearly endeavour to avoid both of these situations if you possibly can.

Nevertheless, there can be many urgent situations where a sales manager is obliged to seek a new job right away, perhaps needing a change of location, escape from an unsatisfactory business relationship, or even to avoid unemployment. So what are the options? Frankly, there aren't very many. One fundamental decision must be the acceptance of a transient drop in status, perhaps by returning into direct sales. Once this mental adjustment has been made, it is important to assess how one's existing skills and experience can be augmented by any new employment, so as to increase one's personal value, and thus employability in the market-place. Efforts to secure further employment should then be directed towards those companies whose success and management philosophy is most likely to offer the best opportunities for returning to a management role.

One perhaps surprising reaction, but regular phenomenon among managers who decide to return to a direct selling role, is that their release from the hassles, politics and insecurity of management responsibility is such a relief, and the relative rewards and satisfaction of being a salesperson so much better than they remembered, that they can see no point in returning to what they previously saw as a challenge and now perceive as an easy route to a premature heart attack!

# Index